4th e-Learning Excellence Awards 2018

An Anthology of Case Histories

Edited by Dan Remenyi

4th e-Learning Excellence Awards 2018: An Anthology of Case Histories

First published October 2018

Note to readers: Some papers have been written by authors who use the American form of spelling and some use the British. These two different approaches have been left unchanged.

ISBN: 978-1-912764-06-8

Printed by Lightning Source POD

Published by: Academic Conferences and Publishing International Limited, Reading, RG4 9SJ, United Kingdom, info@academic-conferences.org

Available from www.academic-bookshop.com

Table of Contents

Acknowledgements

We would like to thank the judges, who initially read the abstracts of the case histories submitted to the competition and discussed these to select those to be submitted as full case histories. They subsequently evaluated the entries and made further selections to produce the finalists who are published in this book.

Dr. Paula Charbonneau-Gowdy received her PhD from McGill University in Montreal, Canada. Since 2011, she has been an Assistant Professor and researcher in English as a Foreign Language Teacher Education at the Universidad Andres Bello in Santiago, Chile. She formerly served as Senior Advisor in Learning and Technology to the Government of Canada where she designed national and international blended and distance language programs. Her research interests lie in traditional and virtual classroom-based research and the socio-cultural implications of emerging technologies on teaching, learning and learners.

Susan Crichton is the Director of the Faculty of Education at the University of British Columbia and the founding director of the Innovative Learning Centre. Her work explores the Maker Movement and the thoughtful design and development of digital learning environments to enable quality teaching and learning, especially in challenging contexts.

Colin Loughlin is Learning Technology Officer at the University of Surrey where his main roles are helping to engage staff with learning technologies through staff development and project work. His research interests include informal learning with social media tools and digital note-taking.

Professor Anabela Mesquita is Professor at ISCAP since 1990. She is Vice Dean, a member of the Agoritmi Center at the Universidade do Minho and the Director of CICE (research centre) (ISCAP).She gained her PhD at Universidade do Minho in Management Information

iii

Systems in 2002. Her research interests include Knowledge and Innovation Management, Impact of Information Systems in Organizations, Life Long Learning at the Higher Education level, Social Media and e-Learning.

Reet Cronk is originally from Australia and currently chairs the Information Systems Department at Harding University USA. She has a multidisciplinary background of medical technology, molecular genetics and information systems. Her most recent research has been in the evaluation of web 2 technology, gamification, e-learning social and intellectual capital, and knowledge sharing.

Dr. Jarmila Novotná is a professor in the Faculty of Education at Charles University in Prague, Czech Republic. Her main fields of interest are didactical conditions of the transformation of students' models of activities when grasping knowledge and skills, pre- and in-service training of mathematics teachers for their profession and transfer of research results into practice. She is author or co-author of several book chapters, articles and textbooks and member of national and international project teams in the field of mathematics education.

Introduction

e-Learning has become such a central part of how we manage the delivery of education and training in the 21st century and the International e-Learning Excellence Awards provides an opportunity for individuals and groups to consider new and innovative ways of using this method of learning.

The response to the fourth e-Learning Excellence Awards has reflected the innovative initiatives in place in many parts of the world. With 27 initial submissions from 12 countries, 20 competitors were invited to send in a full case history describing their initiative. The range of subjects written about in the case histories has certainly been extensive and the panel of expert judges had their job cut out for them to find the most interesting case histories and short list them down to the finalists published in this anthology.

The 14 authors or groups of authors have been invited to present their work at the European Conferences on e-Learning in Athens, Greece in November. The topics which will be addressed are listed in the Contents page of this book.

I would like to thank all the contributors to this book for the excellent work which has been done towards developing new and interesting ways of applying e-Learning. And of course it is also important to thank the individuals who constituted our panel of expert judges.

Dr Dan Remenyi
Editor
October 2018

Teaching to Future e-Learning Experts through Blended Methods

Francesca Amenduni[1] and Maria Beatrice Ligorio[2]
[1]Department of Educational Sciences, University of the Study of Roma Tre, Italy
[2]Department of Education, Psychology and communication, University of the Study "Aldo Moro" Bari, Italy
francesca.amenduni@unifg.it
mariabeatrice.ligorio@uniba.it

Abstract:
Becoming a professional is a process of fusing theoretical and practical aspects (Hytönen et al., 2016). Although university is considered as an elective agency to support students' transition to workplaces, when looking into the university curricula there is no great synergy between academia and work demands (Eteläpelto et al., 2014). We have tried to fill this gap by applying the design principles of the Trialogical Learning Approach – TLA (Paavola & Hakkarainen, 2005) in a master degree course in "Educational and E-learning Psychology" (University of Bari Aldo Moro) with the main aim to support transition between academic and professional communities. Thus, companies relevant in the field of E-learning are involved. A group of students is assigned to each company with the task to contribute to the development of an object the company is creating. In this task, several types of technologies are used: instant messaging, web-forum, Video-calls, project and knowledge management tools. Furthermore, students are required to learn how to design educational videos and learning objects by using software such as Articulate.pro and iMovie. Based on these premises, we have developed a model called Blended Collaborative and Constructive Participation (BCCP), meant specifically for university teaching. Our results showed that students appreciated the opportunity to work in groups and with companies, to use flexible technologies, and to become aware of the e-learning job market. The course had a positive effect on students' self-efficacy and on building professional identity. This research could provide general insights for university courses aimed at supporting transition to workplace.

1. Introduction

Youth unemployment in Italy is among the highest in Europe, especially in the South. Italian graduates with a job after one year are 74% in the North and only 53% in the South. In addition, about 53% of Italian graduates declares that universities training was not useful for their current job.

The NMC report 2017 defines universities as "incubators of high-quality products — actual inventions and developments that progress positive trends, as well as the most important product of all: graduates who not only fulfil evolving job market needs but redefine and improve the workforce they enter". According with this definition, university should be the elective agency supporting students' transition toward workplace. Nevertheless, academia and job-market do not find a good synergy when looking at the university curricula (Eteläpelto et al., 2014; Hytonen et al., 2016). Recently, universities are recognizing this problem and are adopting programs to interconnect universities and workplaces through technologies (Trede et al. 2016). However, this is not the case for most of the Italian universities, characterized by low investment in quality training, innovation and technology, especially in the southern regions.

We are trying to fill this gap by experimenting innovative methods in a master degree course in "Educational and E-learning Psychology", at the University of Bari Aldo Moro, one of the biggest university in the South of Italy. The course aims at preparing Master students interested in E-learning.

Firstly, we looked at the personal resources that could help students in the transition from university to workplaces. We identified the following inter-related personal resources critical for students' employability (Tomlinson, 2012): identity, self-efficacy, personal and professional skills, and perspectives concerning the e-learning job market opportunities.

Then, we looked for a pedagogical approach to develop these resources. We opted for the Trialogical Learning Approach (TLA) that proposes forms of learning based on collaboratively planning, developing and transformation of "shared knowledge objects", by using flexible technologies. TLA emphasizes the cross-fertilization between education and society and the need to involve stakeholders beyond traditional learning contexts so that authentic challenges and experiences can develop innovative knowledge practices (Paavola & Hakkarainen, 2014). The objects built function as transactional medium, accompanying students as they cross the borders between educational and professional contexts. This approach allows trying out professional practices in a protected learning environment. Positive impact has been recorded from both students and teachers side (Lakkala et al. 2015).

2. The infrastructure

Based on these premises, we defined a model called Blended Collaborative and Constructive Participation (BCCP) (Ligorio & Annese, 2010), specifically meant for university teaching. This model does not conceive merely alternation of online and offline learning. Instead, there is cross-fertilization between online and face-to-face interactions.

The 13-week course is divided into two modules: Module 1 covers the curricular content, while Module 2 focuses on activities designed and performed in concert with companies operating in the E-learning market. Module 1 starts with a familiarization phase during which the teacher introduces face-to-face the course and the university tutors. As warming up, students are required to participate to an informal discussion and to open up personal e-portfolio - described later in detail. During the first week, the teacher divides the students into groups – called "expert" groups - of minimum 4 and maximum 10 students. Right after, the teacher selects a number of study materials corresponding to the number of students forming these groups. The initial lecture ends by negotiating a challenging research question, which would guide the subsequent activities. The purpose of setting a research question is to avoid rote learning and trigger a progressive inquiry attitude (Hakkarainein, 2003).

Students download the learning materials from Google Drive and discuss within the expert groups via a web-forum called ForumCommunity, complemented by scheduled face-to-face discussions. Once the "expert" discussion ends, students are individually required to write a brief review using a template provided by the teacher. In these reviews, students highlight content useful to answer to the research question. Once the reviews are ready, they are posted on Google Drive. Now new groups are formed by students coming from different "expert" groups. We call these groups "Jigsaw" groups since this technique is inspired by Aronson (Aronson & Bridgeman, 1979). These groups compare and combine the various answers to the research question, gleaned through the reviews with the aim of collaboratively creating a concept map. This activity takes place again via web-forum into ForumCommunity, interspersed with scheduled face-to-face encounters.

Within both expert and Jigsaw groups, students are required to cover specific roles. Based on the Role Taking theory (Fischer, et al. 2013), these roles are designed to support responsibility taking and active participation. Some of the roles used are: (a) leader of web-forum group discussions – responsible for monitoring assignments and deadlines and checking that all participants are active; (b) collaborative product manager – responsible for preparing a first draft of the collaborative object and soliciting feedback from each participant; (c) researcher – responsible for seeking information useful for the activities.

The following figure synthesis the activities featuring Module 1.

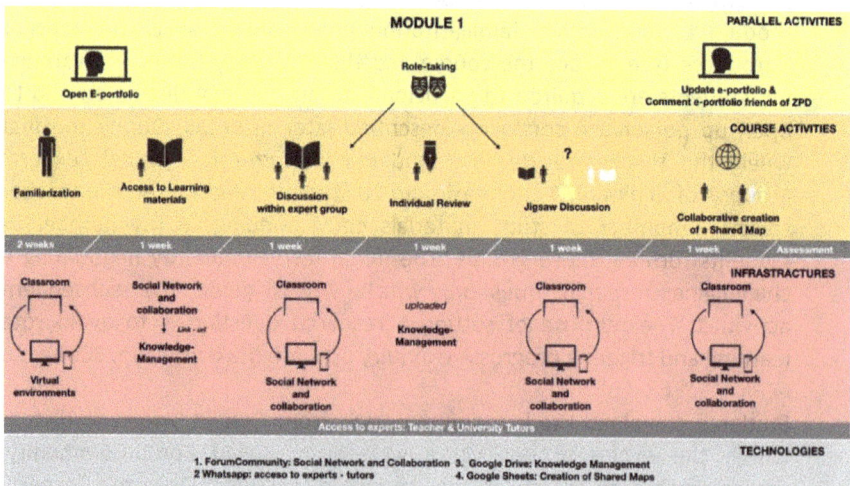

Figure 1: Synopsis of Module 1 structure

About Module 2, the overall goal is to put into practice what was learned in Module 1. To achieve this aim, a group of students is assigned to each company. Entrepreneurs introduced the company via Skype or via webinars or in presence, depending on the possibility and entrepreneurs' preferences. They also describe the object students will participate at the construction of. Again, expert and Jigsaw groups are formed. The expert groups work with the same company, while the Jigsaw groups are composed by students working with different companies. Within the Jigsaw groups, students compare their work and offer reciprocal feedback based on the assessment criteria proposed by the companies. Role-taking was also active in Module 2, with the same roles already experimented in Module 1 and with addition new roles introduced by the companies. The following Figure reports the structure of Module 2.

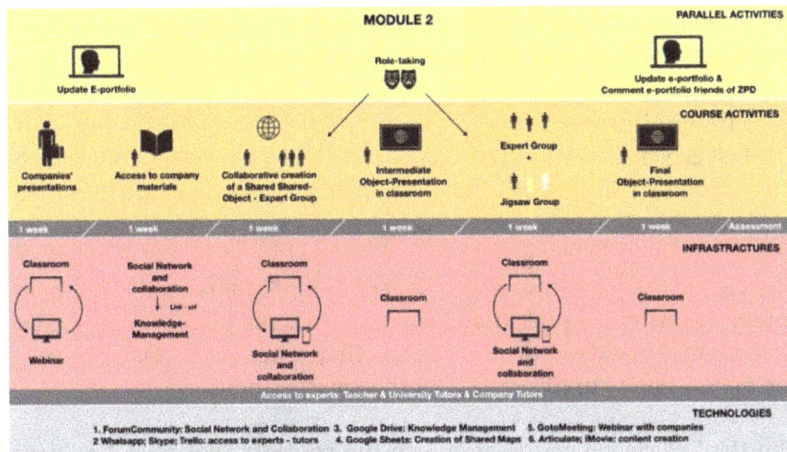

Figure 2: Synopsis of Module 2 structure

Just for illustrative purposes, the following Table provides a description of three of the nine companies involved during the year 2017-18.

Table 1: Description of some of the company involved in the course

Name	Number of company tutors involved	Number of university tutors involved	Area in Italy	Objects built with the participation of the students	Technology used to realise the object and to collaborate with company
Gruppo Pragma	3	2	North	A trailer and a Didactic Unit about AI	iMovie; Articulate Pro; Skype;
Osel	2	2	South	A didactic unit about the company's story	Articulate Pro; Trello.
Entropy	2	2	Centre	A serious game for job interviews	Yammer

Transversally to the modules, students maintain their e-portfolio, first on ForumCommunity and later on LinkedIn. At the outset of the course, students are required to post their expectations about this experience. At the end of each module, students select what they think best represents their performance and fill out a self-assessment sheet. At the end of Module 1, students outline personal goals for Module 2, whilst at the end of Module 2 they summarize the competencies acquired during the course, examine their initial expectations and comment on them. Within their e-portfolio, students were required to invite a 'friend of zone of proximal development' (ZPD) that monitors the activities and gives suggestions for improvements. Clearly inspired by Vygotsky (1978), this role is crucial in supporting dyads interaction and improving e-portfolio quality.

3. The challenges

The first challenge was related to poor technological resources provided by the university institution. No institutional e-learning platform was available; therefore we worked with free devices.

The second challenge concerned the lack of funds for recruiting university tutors. Therefore, we relied on volunteer students from previous course that wanted to extend their expertise. They covered this task as part of their internship or to collect data for their master thesis.

The third challenge was related with the students shift from traditional study strategies to methods typical of workplaces. Initially, students felt stressed about deadline pressure and time-management. For them was also hard to work within so many different groups (four in total). Furthermore, some students did not feel at ease working with technologies and did not trust that real learning could be conveyed. To overcome this aspect, a period of familiarization with the technology was allotted at the outset of the course. Moreover, Module 1 was introduced as a safe warm-up for Module 2, before encountering the companies. In addition, university tutors reported their experience as former students. Some companies hired students from previous courses and they could testify the positive outcome of attending the course, resultant in professional real possibilities.

4. How the initiative was received

We collect opinions through several means with three target groups: students, university tutors and company tutors. Here we will report synthetically the perspective of each of these groups.

Students declared to appreciate improvement of their professional skills (26%), understanding of using digital tools for professional and educational purposes (25%), group-work (22%), collaboration with companies (16%) and construction of usable objects (10%).

When comparing our course to a traditional one of the same faculty (Bruno, 2018), results showed that the perception of usefulness was significantly greater in our course (F (1,101) = 7.76, p <.01) and students considered the blended course more interesting (F (1,101) = 15.21, p <.001).

Provenzano (2018) carried out two focus group discussions with students at the end of the course. Her results confirmed that working with companies was one of the most appreciated aspects and the value of technologies as learning tools was acknowledged. Students recognized the importance of Module 1 as preparation for the practical activities in Module 2. As negative aspects, students report that too short time was allocated to accomplish all the tasks. Zaccaria et al. (2018) focused on the students' perceptions about using webinars. The 94% of participants appreciated the webinar experience and 74% considered it as a good tool to enrich university teaching. The 59% of participants appreciated the opportunity to attend the companies' presentation at a distance, without being physically in the university room.

About tutors' perspectives, the 12 company tutors interviewed all acknowledged the opportunity of a mutual contamination. The 42% of them also appreciated the opportunity to work with students. The 85% declared they improved their understanding of students' personal sources in career-management.

The university tutors (N = 11) appreciated in particular the opportunity to collaborate with companies (64%) and with peers (17%). In addition, they valued the opportunity to professional skills (58%), tutoring practices (38%) and E-learning knowledge (18%).

5. The learning outcomes

In the following table, outcomes and assessment methods are summarized.

Table 2: Outcomes and assessment methods

General resources	Specific resources	Data collected from	Target group
Personal resources	Identity (I-Positioning)	Student and Professional e-portfolio self-description	Students,
	Self-efficacy	CKP questionnaire	
	Development of personal and professional skills	Focus-group; Companies Questionnaire;	Students; Company tutors.
	Perspective of Job Market opportunities	Focus-Group	Students.

First of all, we looked at students' e-portfolio to track down the identity trajectory from university to workplace (Amenduni & Ligorio, 2017). Three different I-positions have been singled out: monological (stressing individual perspective); dialogical (considering the collaborative dimension); and trialogical (including the shared objects). By comparing ForumCommunity and LinkedIn e-portfolio, we found that trialogical positions occurred more in the second one. This shows that for the students the object built is a "proof" of their professional identity, to be shared in a public and professional space such as LinkedIn. Monological and dialogical positions are very frequent in ForumCommunity.

We also looked at the effect of the friend of ZPD (Impedovo et al, 2018) and we found that it promotes the emergence of professional I-positions. Secondly, we analysed the perception of self-efficacy by using the CKP – Contextual Knowledge Practices Questionnaire (Mukkonen, et al., 2017). Comparing self-efficacy before and after the course, it was recorded a significant increase (t(17)= 4.51, p<.001).

Thirdly, we analysed students' self-perceptions of skills acquisitions. During the focus group discussions, students claimed that the Module 2 allowed them to develop relational and transversal skills (the most quoted skills were mediation, negotiation and communication). Company tutors had the same perceptions: the course positively affected communicative, transversal and collaborative skills. Students also declared they acquired digital skills and they considered new professional horizons concerning E-learning. Finally, they also understood the relationship between their skills, their training paths and future job opportunities.

6. Plans to further develop the initiative;

To understand how the BCC model can evolve, at each edition, we collect suggestions from students, companies, researchers, and university tutors. The following table summarizes the insights received and how we intent to implement them in the next edition.

Table 3: Suggestions and future developments

Stakeholders	Suggestions	Further developments
Students	Less pressure time. No assessment of the informal activities such as e-portfolio and organizational discussions. More time allocated to work with the companies	Module 1 will be shortened Assessment will be based on products and activities connected to the construction of them
Companies	They would like to collect more information about individual students.	At the end of the course students will be required to produce an individual self-presentation (as video, story-telling, etc.) describing their personal contribution to the object and their skills to be shared with the companies
Researchers	Multi-disciplinary teams are more efficient.	We will create partnerships with other universities in order to create multi-disciplinary teams who work around shared objects committed by e-learning company
University tutors	It is hard to track down each students participation through all the digital tools used during the course. It would be good to have a way for a faster and more efficient way to perform this task	We will look for platforms that help tutors tracking students performances automatically (e.g. Learning Analytics).

References

Amenduni, F., & Ligorio, M. B. (2017). Becoming at the borders: the role of positioning in boundary-crossing between university and workplaces. Cultural-Historical Psychology, 13(1), 89-104.

Aronson, E., & Bridgeman, D. (1979). Jigsaw groups and the desegregated classroom: In pursuit of common goals. Personality and social psychology bulletin, 5(4), 438-446.

Bruno E. (2018). Misurare l'efficacia di un corso universitario blended. In Ubique e intelligenti: tecnologie e persone. VI Congresso CKBG Collaborative Knowledge Building Group.

Eteläpelto, A., Vähäsantanen, K., Hökkä, P., & Paloniemi, S. (2014). Identity and agency in professional learning. In International handbook of research in professional and practice-based learning (pp. 645-672). Springer, Dordrecht.

Fischer, F., Kollar, I., Stegmann, K., & Wecker, C. (2013). Toward a script theory of guidance in computer-supported collaborative learning. Educational psychologist, 48(1), 56-66.

Hakkarainen, K. A. I. (2003). Emergence of progressive-inquiry culture in computer-supported collaborative learning. Learning Environments Research, 6(2), 199-220.

Hytönen, K., Palonen, T., Lehtinen, E., & Hakkarainen, K. (2016). Between two advisors: interconnecting academic and workplace settings in an emerging field. Vocations and Learning, 9(3), 333-359.

Impedovo, M.A.; Ligorio, M.B.; McLay, K.F. (2018). The "friend of zone of proximal development" role: Empowering ePortfolios as boundary objects from student to-work I-position transaction. Journal of Assisted Computer Learning

Lakkala, M., Toom, A., Ilomäki, L., & Muukkonen, H. (2015). Re-designing university courses to support collaborative knowledge creation practices. Australasian Journal of Educational Technology (Online Edition).

Ligorio, M. B., & Annese, S. (2010). Blended activity design approach. A method for innovating e-learning communities in higher education. RowińskiT.(Ed.), Blachnio, A., Przepiorka, & AMA Internet in Psychological Research.

Muukkonen, H., Lakkala, M., Toom, A., & Ilomäki, L. (2017). Assessment of competences in knowledge work and object-bound collaboration during higher education courses. Higher Education Transitions: Theory and Research, 288-305.

Paavola, S., & Hakkarainen, K. (2014). Trialogical approach for knowledge creation. In Knowledge creation in education (pp. 53-73). Springer, Singapore.

Provenzano C. (2018) Blended learning in un contesto universitario: la percezione dell'efficacia da parte degli studenti. In Ubique e intelligenti: tecnologie e persone. VI Congresso CKBG Collaborative Knowledge Building Group.

Tomlinson, M. (2012). Graduate employability: A review of conceptual and empirical themes. Higher Education Policy, 25(4), 407-431.

Trede, F., Goodyear, P., Macfarlane, S., Markauskaite, L., McEwen, C., & Tayebjee, F. (2016). Enhancing Workplace Learning through Mobile Technology: Barriers and Opportunities to the Use of Mobile Devices on Placement in the Healthcare and Education Fields. Mobile Learning Futures–Sustaining Quality Research and Practice in Mobile Learning, 250.

Zaccaria M., Di Maso R., Amenduni F., Ligorio M. B., (2018). Quando l'e-learning diventa professionalizzante. In Non solo Webinar, Progedit.

Contributing Author Biographies

Francesca Amenduni is a PhD Student in Experimental Pedagogy. Her expertise is in the e-learning field both as practitioner and researcher. She has worked as e-learning tutor and instructional designer since 2015. She carried research related to blended learning and her current PhD project regards semi-automated assessment of Critical Thinking in e-learning forums.

Maria Beatrice Ligorio is a full Professor in Educational Psychology. She has a PhD in Psychology of Communication. Her research concerns collaborative learning, socio-constructivism, identity, e-learning and blended learning. She has several experiences as member of the executive committee of international scientific organizations such as EARLI and ISCAR and she is currently the main editor of the Qwerty Journal.

eConcordia: Implementation of Gamification in Online Courses

Robert Beauchemin[1], Antonia Tripa[2] and Nishan Joomun[3]
[1]CEO KnowledgeOne/eConcordia, Canada
[2]Director of Innovation, and Business Development
[3]VP IT, and Development
robert.beauchemin@knowledgeone.ca
antonia.tripa@knowledgeone.ca
nishan.joomun@knowledgeone.ca

Abstract
Gamification is shaping up to be one of the leading trends in elearning, increasing participation and social interactions in online courses. Research shows that proper integration of gamified components can create a positive impact on the learning process, leading to higher satisfaction, motivation and greater engagement of students. Exploring new ways of creating engagement in our courses, we transformed Concordia University's Introduction to Astronomy course into a gamified experience, using our proprietary game engine. Throughout their learning experience, students answer course-related questions and earn coordinates and fuel cells that allow them to explore new worlds, in a fantasy story that unravels on their screens, based on their assignments results. The Coordinates are allotted via lesson knowledge checks, while the Fuel Cells are allotted via end-of-lesson quizzes. The fantasy story – Space Odyssey – is a non-graded component of the course, that not only sends the students on a journey of finding a suitable planet for a dying Earth population but also creates a competitive environment where they compete among themselves to place higher on the Leaderboard. This course provides an introduction to major topics in astronomy. The journey begins with a description of our planet, its place in the solar system, and resulting seasonal changes, tidal movements, and earth's precession. Farther out, the solar system, the planets, star clusters, the Milky Way galaxy, and remote systems such as black holes and supernovae are explored. Pairing the gamification elements with media-intensive and interactive web content transformed this course into an engaging experience, student course completion surveys pointing out to the successful implementation of this approach.
Further information: https://youtu.be/zgo_wJK6B0w

1. Introduction

PHYS 284 - Introduction to Astronomy is one of the courses offered to undergraduate students, at Concordia University in Montreal, Canada. Open to all students interested in space, the course provides an introduction to major topics in astronomy. This course is primarily (70%) about facts of Astronomy. No prior knowledge of mathematics or physics is required. Every concept is described from basic principles, and although mathematical formulas are occasionally mentioned, the student is only required to understand the qualitative nature of a formula and is not expected to perform arithmetic calculations in this course. In addition to facts, the student is required to apply mental concepts (30%) from mathematical and physical notions to form judgments about concepts in Astronomy (for example, whether a star is visible in the northern hemisphere given its celestial coordinates).

Offered in class until 2016, the course was moved to an online format to take advantage of a medium that is more suitable for simulations, and animations of different space phenomena. As main learning objective, the course aims to develop in students critical thinking about news relating to space science and discoveries, helping them understand better our place in the Universe and master the core subject material. The goal to think critically (and quantitatively at the same time) focuses on making students able not just to solve fixed problems, but also to transform complex space phenomena into well-formulated questions.

Gamifying this course allowed us to create a learning environment that led students to engage better with the content and offered us a stepping-stone into integrating similar approaches in other online courses.

2. The infrastructure

The initial team involved three main groups, as follows:

- Online Pedagogy – led by a Learning Advisor with a solid background in Educational Technology
- Technology – led by a Technology Expert with a solid background in User Experience and IT Development
- Subject Matter – the professor teaching the course in-class

The course was deployed using our Learning Management System (LMS), a proprietary software application built over the course of the last 18 years.

Having an in-house system, which is created using .NET framework and SQL Server, allows us to easily customize the content's visual representation. As such, we are not limited to the linear style of presentation that is prevalent with off-the-shelf systems (i.e., Moodle).

All the streaming videos are hosted internally, and the delivery platform is Adobe Media Server supporting both HLS and HDS protocols.

Our courses are hosted at two (2) Datacenters. They provide a full redundancy; in case that one fails, the traffic automatically switches to the other one with minimal service interruption. In addition, each one has an F5 load balancer that distributes the traffic on four (4) webservers, thus minimizing the stress and ensuring better server-side performance.

Beside the .NET gamification engine, the content is produced using two (2) authoring tools:

- Adobe Captivate for the lectures
- iSpring for the quizzes

All the tracking is done using a third-party platform, SCORM Cloud, with the latest xAPI standards. The textbook of the course resides on Texidium, and the integration is done via the LTI protocol, which provides seamless accessibility for the user, no other login being required. Discussions between students are supported via Instaforum Discussion Board, while the virtual sessions held by the instructor and teaching assistants are done using Adobe Connect.

3. The challenges

Moving the content to an online medium came with the challenge of creating an interactive experience that would keep the students engaged in the program, throughout the semester. In the same time, the professor wanted to break certain misconceptions related to the field of Astronomy, making students understand better course-related concepts, regardless of their educational background.

In order to address the latter, we implemented, for each course module, a poll that was challenging certain misconceptions about the Universe. As students answered questions, they could compare their beliefs with those of other students, creating a social scale of certain mistaken views.

Test your misconceptions

Can we see the Milky Way Galaxy in the night sky?

⦿ **a) Yes**
    72% of participants answered this.

○ **b) No**
    28% of participants answered this.

Feedback

Correct! On a clear night, the Milky Way can be seen as a cloud of dust extending from one part of the sky to the opposite end.

Results based on 822 participants.
Revisit regularly to see the class' tendencies, as participation increases. | **1/3** | ⇨

In order to involve students better in the course, we transformed the material into a gamified experience, using our proprietary game engine. Pairing the gamification elements with media-intensive and interactive web content transformed this course into an engaging experience, student course completion surveys pointing out to the successful implementation of this approach. It is important to mention that the game is supporting and not driving or interfering with the learning. Thus a student could experience the course without getting involved into the game.

The final solution was developed around three main points:

1. Side story – providing students with a fantasy trip through the Universe

During their learning journey, students answer course-related questions and earn coordinates and fuel cells that allow them to explore new worlds, in a fantasy story that unravels on their screens. This story has two levels, one focusing on finding different planets in the Universe and the second exploring these planets and assessing if they are suitable for life. A preface of the story is presented at the beginning of each semester, with the rest of it being locked, pending the completion of a certain number of challenges and accumulating enough rewards to proceed to the next chapter.

The two types of rewards are allotted via two different types of assessments per lesson; lecture knowledge checks and end-of-lesson quizzes. Thus, there are:

- Two (2) levels of quizzes per lesson; one on fundamental concepts and one on advanced concepts, through which coordinates can be earned, and
- Ten (10) knowledge checks per lesson through which fuel cells can be earned.

Coordinates

- Six (6) coordinates are required to travel to the next destination of the story
- Coordinates are earned by passing the quizzes at the end of each lesson with a grade of 60% or higher.

- Fundamental quizzes earn students two (2) coordinates each
- Advanced quizzes earn students one (1) coordinate each
- Each lesson will provide students with a chance to earn up to three (3) coordinates

Fuel Cells

- Six (6) fuel cells are required to explore locations, once they have been unveiled by the awarded coordinates
- Fuel cells are earned by correctly answering knowledge check questions at the end of lecture sections
- Knowledge check questions do not count towards students' final grade
- Each lesson will provide students with a chance to earn up to 10 fuel cells

2. Leaderboard

Students have access at all time to a Leaderboard, seeing their progression through the story and comparing their achievements with those of their peers. This was done to increase engagement in the course through social comparisons.

The leaderboards are updated continuously making sure that no out-of-date data or rankings are shown, and provide users with a sense of progress and gratification. Students have to pick a nickname while playing the game; therefore, the ranking does not display students' actual names.

Apart from the Leaderboard, a Peer Activity Page was created, where students can view, in real-time, the game activities/achievement of all participating students (this page is one of the most visited pages in the game, based on traffic analytics).

For every coordinate they achieve, students earned 1 point on the leaderboard. The same value applied to every fuel cell earned.

3. Course graphic design

Considering the exciting field of Astronomy, it was mandatory for us to create an immersive experience, which relied, apart from a sound pedagogy, on visually engaging content. This allowed us not only to create a stimulating experience but provided students with enough resources to be able to easily recognize space phenomena, in different contexts.

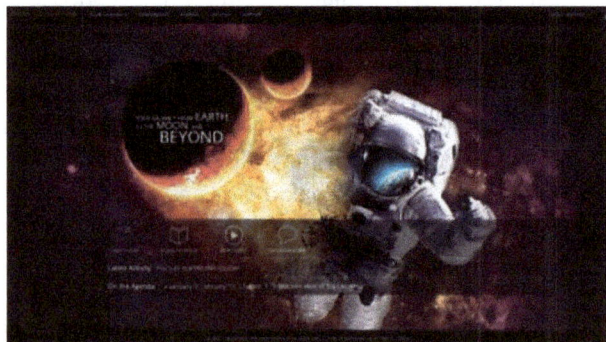

4. How the initiative was received

Every one of our courses has an end-of-semester evaluation survey. Through this, we gauge the students' feedback on the course content, technology, professors and teaching assistants, and different course components. This allows us not only to revise certain concepts presented in the course but also to improve constantly on our technology and course design. Some of the comments received pointed out the engaging nature of the online course and the overall design:

"The thing I enjoyed the most was the subject and how it was presented to someone like me. I'm not of a scientific mind, but this course made science comprehensible and easy to understand. It was extremely enjoyable despite all the hard work and I will endeavor to continue studying this subject matter at my own pace."

"I loved the overall design, easily the best online class I ever took. The effort that went into designing the lessons and interface is very noticeable. The Teaching Assistants and Professor were very easy to interact with as well."

"Not a physics student but I loved this class. Always interested in astronomy and I loved how interactive this class was."

"The layout and design made it enjoyable and inviting to go on the course website. The weekly quizzes, videos and the game were the best way that I have seen to make an online class dynamic."

"Normally I would always keep my work till the last minute, but due to the game mechanics, I've been putting way more effort into completing quizzes and lessons ahead of time, as well as studying harder for the quizzes. Great job and it's much appreciated! I showed the game system to all my friends."

89% of respondents agreed or strongly agreed that the course was an excellent experience for them, with 94% considered that their knowledge of the subject matter has increased as a result of this course. 90% would recommend the course to others.

Some of the challenges encountered by students were related to accessing the course content on different browsers, with IPad Pro's Safari having a few issues in displaying the content properly. These issues were addressed during the first course offering.

Other students would have liked to have the course content available on a mobile device. However, due to the amount of information, the length of some of the lectures and the interactions required from students it has been decided to optimize the course content only down to a tablet device size. Limitations from the authoring tools used played a factor in this decision as well.

5. The course outcomes
One of the major outcomes of the integration of gamified components in the online course was the level of student engagement achieved. Our LMS allows us to track the students' interactions with the course content throughout the semester. This permitted us to compare these interactions with others made in regular online courses void of gamified components. Our online courses are structured following the University's in-class courses, with assessments having similar due dates. If generally, students were waiting to complete their assignments on the last day before the deadline (80%-95%), implementing the gamification components created a more engaged audience. In less than twenty-four (24) hours since the course was launched four (4) top achievers already passed through the content of Lesson 1 (students have one week to complete it) and successfully answered the associated quizzes. In total 45% of the assignments were completed at least three (3) days before the due date.

6. Plans to further develop the initiative.
The successful run of the gamified online course led us to the implementation of comparable approaches in other online courses. A similar gamified experience was successfully implemented in a course teaching Old English through the works of J.R.R. Tolkien. For this specific course a side story was developed, focusing on the life and death of the dragon Smaug, one of the characters in Tolkien's The Hobbit. Similar to the Introduction to Astronomy approach, students unveil different chapters in the story by correctly answering course-related questions. In the same time, they accumulate badges and advance in the course leaderboard.

We also integrated game components in other online courses were the gamified experience blended with the integration of online collaboration tools (created on Twitter API). Students are placed on the Leaderboards based on the number and quality of the interactions between them.

References:

Marko Urh, Goran Vukovic, Eva Jereb, Rok Pintar (2015,) The Model for Introduction of Gamification into E-learning in Higher Education; Procedia - Social and Behavioral Sciences Volume 197, 25 July 2015

Contributing Author Biographies

Robert Beauchemin leads the academic and commercial development of eConcordia / KnowledgeOne. Working closely with the Board of Directors, Robert leads the company in developing solutions and strategies that meet the evolving needs of the modern digital world, while expanding the organisation's reputation from locally to nationally and internationally – forging sustainable partnerships along the way with key stakeholders in the academic community, relevant business, and government constituencies. Before joining KnowledgeOne in 2014, Robert was Vice President of the Global Training and Simulation Division and led the Knowledge Management group for ten years at SNC-Lavalin. For more than 30 years, Robert actively participates in the design and deployment of training solutions dedicated to learning, using advanced technologies. These projects are implemented in North and South America, in Europe and Africa.

Antonia Tripa is a 2016 award-winning innovator of the International E-Learning Association for her gamification mandate in higher education. She is currently responsible for the strategy behind KnowledgeOne's high-stakes contracts, the foundation of an innovation hub, and the creation, selling, and management of a new era of consultation services. Antonia has over seven years of experience in training and education, including consultation experience in a variety of fields, such as agro-foods, transportation, construction, health and safety, and higher education.

Nishan Joomun leads eConcordia / KnowledgeOne's Development and IT team. His mandate is to implement innovative and cutting-edge solutions that will position the company as a leader and trendsetter in the eLearning world. A graduate of Cambridge University, Nishan has more than 20 years in the field, and his work has won many prestigious awards including the Canadian Digi awards, Canadian

Network for Innovation in Education, IELA and many more. Nishan is a renowned speaker and has more than a dozen sessions under his belt at some high-profile eLearning conferences like eLearning guild, and ATD.

Fashion Students Choose How to Learn

Michaella Cavanagh
Department of Fashion and Textiles, Durban University of Technology, South Africa
michaellag@dut.ac.za

Abstract:
Incorporating technology into learning a practical subject such as pattern making in a meaningful and authentic way is challenging even in an ideal situation. This is amplified when students come from diverse technology backgrounds. There was a need to blend technology into practical learning while allowing equal access and actively developing students' pattern making skills. In groups, students created videos that explained how to construct a pattern for an assigned sleeve. They had to explain their process, producing knowledge and becoming the teacher. This fostered a deeper understanding of the content, but also gave students agency in deciding the solution and presentation of the process. Although all groups could use the document camera and video editing software installed on the campus computers, they were allowed to record and edit the video however they wanted. Each group was assigned a different style and this allowed more styles to be explored than if taught traditionally. Students watched all the videos and commented through an online discussion forum. They had to critically analyse the videos and give constructive feedback. To cement learning, students were individually assigned a sleeve style (not from their video) and created a poster that explained how to draft the pattern. The most correct posters were selected for each style and uploaded onto the learning management system as notes for all students. Students enjoyed being producers of knowledge and were more engaged in the process than other learning tasks. Groups used different methods to show that there were many 'right' answers. Making videos helped them become more proficient digital citizens. This project has developed over several iterations, but it is only with the addition of the 'poster' that students really acknowledged how much they had learnt. Having the notes that they had created gave them confidence in further projects.

1. Introduction

Before beginning, please view samples of the project at the below links as this might provide more insight into what students were able to achieve:
https://youtu.be/xexrozcinT8
https://youtu.be/EovVpUurljUk

Fashion is a vocational discipline, and students need to know how to use the discipline content in practical and diverse ways (Dall'Alba 2009). When I first began teaching, I taught the way I was taught as a student. Much of this teacher-centred style was demonstrations and lectures, and then asking students to replicate exactly what they had been shown. Reflecting on this, I found that students were able to replicate what had been taught but were unable to apply what they had learnt in other ways. This was especially clear in the sleeves module, where five sleeve styles were demonstrated and replicated by students, but most students struggled to understand how to apply this knowledge practically to other styles of sleeves with similar features.

To help students learn deeply, so that they could understand and apply their knowledge, I needed to change the way that the content was taught. I found the concept of constructive alignment (Biggs 2014) helpful in redesigning the assessment. Biggs (2014) calls for teachers to focus on what students need to be able to do at the completion of an assessment, to ensure that the actual learning outcome is being assessed and not a peripheral skill such as memorising or parroting information. I realised that I was merely teaching students to mimic me and assessing their ability to do so, not their understanding of the content nor their ability to apply it.

To create an aligned assessment that enabled students to learn more deeply, I used Herrington, Oliver and Reeves's (2010) authentic learning characteristics to guide my assessment design. Authentic learning projects help students contextualise knowledge, making it more meaningful and easier to retrieve in different situations. In this initiative, I attempted to redesign my sleeves module assessment to be messy, entangled, closer to real world situations, and open to multiple correct answers and methods (Herrington et al.2010). By doing so, I allowed students to shift from passive knowledge consumers to active knowledge producers.

In order to help students take on a more active role, I made use of technology mediated learning in different forms throughout the assessment interspersed with practical hand work to ensure the best blended experience. The revised project asked students to get into small groups and create videos which explained how to make the pattern for an assigned sleeve (each group was assigned a different sleeve style - see Appendix 1 for examples). They recorded themselves physically creating the pattern for the sleeve they were assigned. This showed them that there were multiple correct answers and helped them discover the answer rather than learn it by route. As part of a feedforward strategy, student-groups were put into teams consisting of two or three groups. These teams watched the videos in progress and gave feedback on how it could be improved in time for each group to make the changes before submitting their final video. The final videos were shared as YouTube links on the learning management system (Blackboard) discussion boards by students themselves and allowed students to give each other feedback and respond to others. The videos were all watched as a class and discussed in the final lesson. After watching the videos, students were individually assigned a different sleeve style to create a 'cheat sheet' poster which explains how to make the pattern for that style. There were 13 different sleeve styles that would be helpful for students to know, and from the basic knowledge of how to make these styles, they would be able to create an infinite variety of different types of sleeves. As there are between 50 – 60 students in each cohort group, each style was assigned to more than one student across the cohort. The 'cheat sheets' which were most correct were scanned in and uploaded to Blackboard for students to access as notes.

This blended approached aimed primarily at creating deeper more authentic learning, but also at engaging students as co-producers of knowledge with agency to choose how they learnt.

2. The infrastructure

The largest section of this intervention was the creation of the video (please see YouTube links provided above, or screen shots in Appendix 4 and 5). Students were allowed to choose who they wanted to work with, getting into groups of two or three. In order to give students freedom and complete creative control, they were allowed to use any method of recording and any software to edit the videos. There were no restrictions on how the video was made, as long as it showed how to make the sleeve pattern clearly and was between three and five minutes long. The freedom students were given was an important motivator, they got very excited to be their own directors and the stars in their own videos. However, these students were in first year and most of them had never made a video before.

I teach at a University of Technology in South Africa, where many of the students are from rural and peri-rural areas. The reality is that many of our students have had very limited experience even using a mouse, while others come to us techno-savvy. This diversity in skill level creates a challenge when asking students to complete technology-mediated tasks. This is also exasperated when students come from very different financial backgrounds, and in one class some students have the latest MacBooks while others do not own a smartphone.

We are fortunate on my campus to have dedicated computer labs that students can access, campus wide Wi-Fi, computers in the library and laptops that students can borrow from the library for a few hours at a time. The resources are available to all students, and this helps to mitigate the gaps between students with their own devices and Wi-Fi at home, and those students without. My classroom is equipped with a Smartboard, that comes with a touch screen panel, projector and document camera. The document camera can record video directly onto a USB thumb drive without the need for any specialised software or hardware.

These resources were important for allowing all students to participate equally – students were able to choose to use the document camera and the video editing software installed on the lab computers if they wanted to. This meant that even students without high end smart phones or cameras could create quality videos. Students themselves were very resourceful, some using their cellphones or laptops, borrowing cameras from family or friends, or making use of the document camera.

Recording the video proved easier than anticipated for most, however, more help was needed when editing the videos. As mentioned before, free video editing software was installed in one of the computer labs and students were able to use this. At the initial briefing, I showed students an overview of how to edit their videos using this software (the basics of cutting, speeding up, adding titles, etc.), but also gave them options of other free software they could use. Our departmental IT Technician was very important during this project, helping students use the software or set up the document camera as needed. Putting students into groups also mitigated the technological disparity, as most of the time, at least one member of the group was comfortable with technology. Some students used the free software on their laptops (iMovie, Shotcut or Microsoft Movie Maker) and some even managed to edit their videos on their cell phones. All students, however, had the option of using the departmental computers.

This project also helped teach students how to become digital citizens, as they were required to have their own YouTube accounts and upload the videos as 'unlisted' onto their accounts. Interestingly, all students had a Google account already, and they used this to login to YouTube. Some students (the minority) already had YouTube channels. I put clear and easy to follow instructions on how to upload their videos in both the virtual (Blackboard) and physical classroom. Students were also asked to email me their YouTube links so that I could verify that the links worked and that there were no problems with accessing the video. Once any issues had been sorted, students were to post these links on the Blackboard discussion forum where their peers could comment, and they could interact (see Appendix 6 and 7). These discussion forum interactions were graded on the Blackboard system (see Appendix 8), and this ensured participation.

3. The challenges
In the first instance of this project, students were asked to make the videos and then save them onto a USB thumb drive in order to transfer onto a lab computer to play for all students. One student had picked up a virus and transferred it to the computer, corrupting all other files. Luckily all students had backups and no work was lost. The following year, I asked students to email me the videos where I would upload them onto YouTube. Not only were these files very large (most too big for email), but uploading proved time consuming for me and many students did not understand how to export their final videos, sending me the project file without the linked videos or in formats I could not open without the software. The following iteration, I asked students to upload the videos onto their own YouTube channels. This worked surprisingly well, and only a

few students needed extra guidance to do this (which I was able to offer in class, though consultation outside of class or over email).

Initially, I found that students were leaving the filming of the video to the last minute and therefore had no time to complete the editing (in itself a time-consuming process). To help, I initiated the peer feedforward session where students were given a critique on their progress by other students. This meant that they had a work-in-progress deadline to work towards in order to have something to show. This was also helpful in giving students feedback in time for students to make positive changes. Many students were advised on different lighting, music, adding voice overs, speeding up or slowing down, all of which were helpful in the creation of their final video. To ensure students actually listened to the advice they were given, I incorporated a mark for whether they had followed the feedback or not. I gave all groups feedback sheets where they wrote structured critiques (with guiding questions such as "what is good about this work?" and "what do you suggest to improve this work?") for each group. I make copies of these before giving them back to the students and referred back to them when assessing. This seemed to help, as students were given the opportunity to change their videos before the bulk of the mark was given.

After the first few iterations of this project, students commented to me that they felt as though they hadn't really 'learnt' sleeves, as many of the student-made videos were wrong, or at least, students did not know which ones were correct. I explained that the project covered many more styles than the syllabus required and that they didn't need to know well off by heart how to do each one, but rather they needed to know how to figure out the best way to get there. However, this comment made me realise that students did not feel that they had learnt despite the fact that I could see in their consequential work that they had. This led to the introduction of the 'cheat sheet' (see Appendix 2 for an example). The 'cheat sheet' was a poster explaining how to do a particular style of sleeve. This was an individual exercise and it contributed 25% of the final mark. I selected 13 common sleeve styles that students should know how to do and assigned each student one of these designs. This meant that each design was done by more than one student. The student poster which showed the most correct method in the clearest way was scanned and uploaded (with my comments on any corrections) onto the Blackboard classroom. A colour photostat was also stuck up in the classroom. These became the students' notes, and now they had 'proof' that they had learnt something and these posters could be 'trusted' because they had been vetted by me.

This 'cheat sheet' was also helpful in addressing the age-old problem of group work. Despite having a peer assessment of each other, and having a peer-group assessment of the final work as well as the work in progress, students were frequently having issues with their group members. This portion counted 25% of the mark and was individual work, so 'lazy' students would not be carried and hardworking students would not be penalised by a difficult group.

4. How the initiative was received
Although a lot of work, students do seem to enjoy this project. They were excited at the briefing and immediately began thinking of creative approaches to making the videos. They enjoyed making the videos themselves and being on camera. They also acknowledged in conversations that the really felt they understood the sleeve that they had been assigned (and for those who didn't, they commented that it showed in the video).

This project has been brought up positively in the annual lecturer and subject quality surveys since the first iteration of the project. Students have said they enjoyed it, asked for more interactive projects like this and said that they preferred making their own videos to watching videos I had made for them. This shows me that they were engaged and actively participating during this project, and that this engagement enhanced their learning experience.

5. The learning outcomes
On completion of the module, students needed to know how to construct and adapt a variety of sleeve styles. After the project, they had been exposed to video instructions of between 14 – 19 styles of sleeves (depending on the number of groups in the cohort). Further, they had made a video showing how to do one style (and to teach others something requires a greater degree of understanding) and an individual 'cheat sheet' poster of a completely different style, gaining mastery of at least two styles. The posters and videos would allow them to construct a much greater number of sleeves than the traditional lecturer-centered approach could, and they would have more authentic understanding of this content.

The videos were assessed on four categories: Clarity, Accuracy, Pattern Process and Presentation. For an example of the feedback given, please refer to Appendix 3. The project also included marks for peer feed-forward and how this was applied in the final video, peer assessment of the video (completed on Blackboard discussion forums), group assessment (students rated each other's group work) and the individual 'cheat sheet'.

6. Plans to further develop the initiative

Students enjoyed being active participants of their own learning. Going forward, I will continue with this project, but hope to find more ways to bring authentic learning into my other modules so that students may learn more actively and deeply.

References:

Biggs, J. 2014. Constructive alignment in university teaching. HERDSA Review of Higher Education, 1(1): 5-22.

Dall'Alba, G. 2009. Learning professional ways of being: Ambiguities of becoming. Educational Philosophy and Theory 41 (1) 34-45.

Herrington, J., Oliver, R., & Reeves, T.C. 2010. A guide to authentic e-learning. Routledge, London and New York.

Appendices

Appendix 1

Examples of the style cards given to students. Each card had a technical drawing of a different sleeve.

Appendix 2

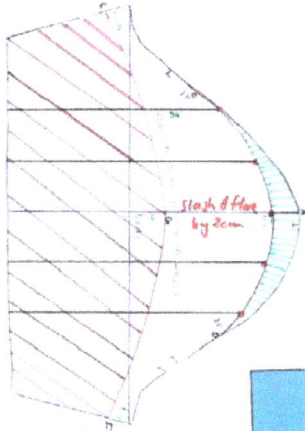

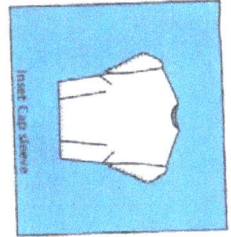

An example of a 'cheat sheet' poster. This page included the style picture, the master pattern and style analysis as well as instructions on how to construct this pattern.

Appendix 3

SLEEVES 2017: Video (Trumpet)		
Clarity: how easy is it to understand the process? Love that you started by analyzing the TD and explained why you did each step. Easy to follow your steps, easy to see. The bit about the 20º angle part was slightly confusing, but not too bad.	25	22
Accuracy: will your video instructions produce the same sleeve as on your TD? Apart from the seam lengths not matching, yes.	25	21
Pattern process: does the tutorial follow the correct pattern process? If closing the dart, you needed to draw the cut line (for the new hem) parallel to the dart arm so that the side seams stay the same length once close.	25	21
Presentation: how well is the information presented? Nice and clean. Music was very appropriate. Jokes were a nice touch. Video and voice over were very clear. A little bit of background noise.	25	21
SUB TOTAL:	100	85
FEEDFORWARD: Stablise footage, music is distracting, make sure footage isn't cropped, smooth camera focus and zoom, get music without lyrics, expand time for berry joke.	10	8.25
HOW IT WAS APPLIED: You have made all suggested changes.	10	10
PEER ASSESSMENT (on Blackboard):	10	

An example of the rubric used to assess the project. This would be given to the group and does not include the individual portions such as the cheat sheet and group member evaluation.

Appendix 4

FLARE AND PASTE, MAKING SURE THE HEM IS STRAIGHT

Screenshot from one of the student made videos

Appendix 5

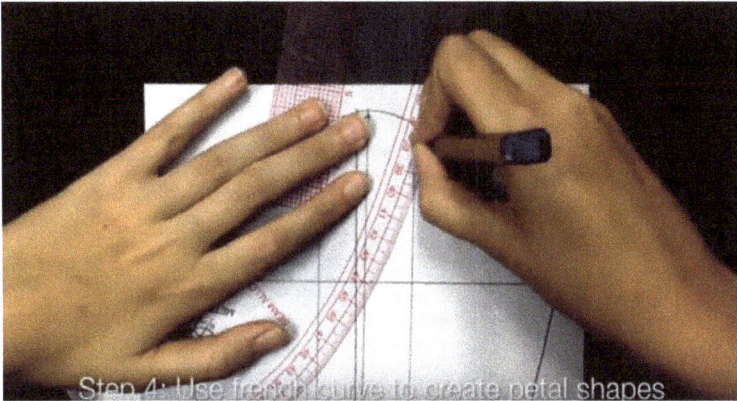

Screenshot from one of the student made videos

Appendix 6

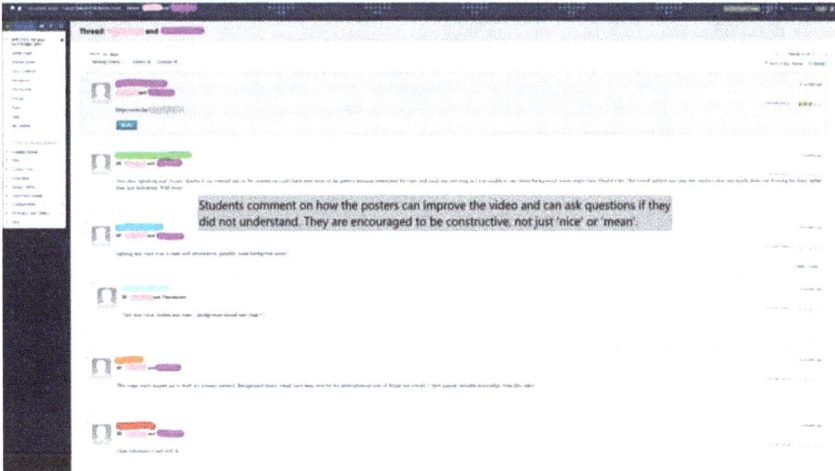

Screenshot from one of the online discussion forum posts

Michaella Cavanagh

Appendix 7

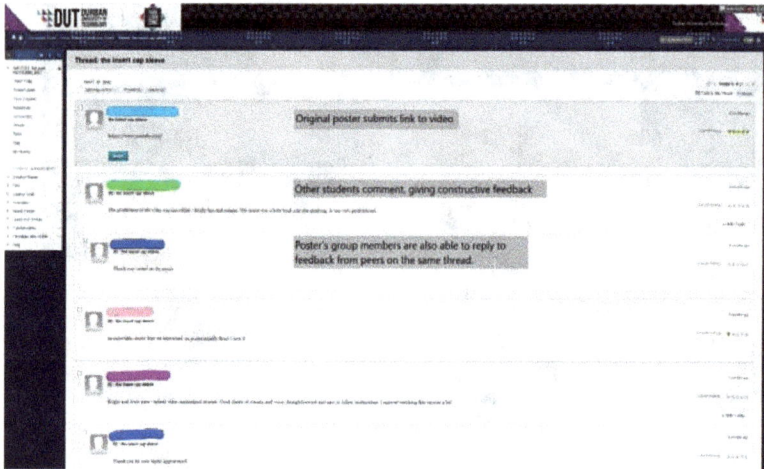

Screenshot from one of the online discussion forum posts

Appendix 8

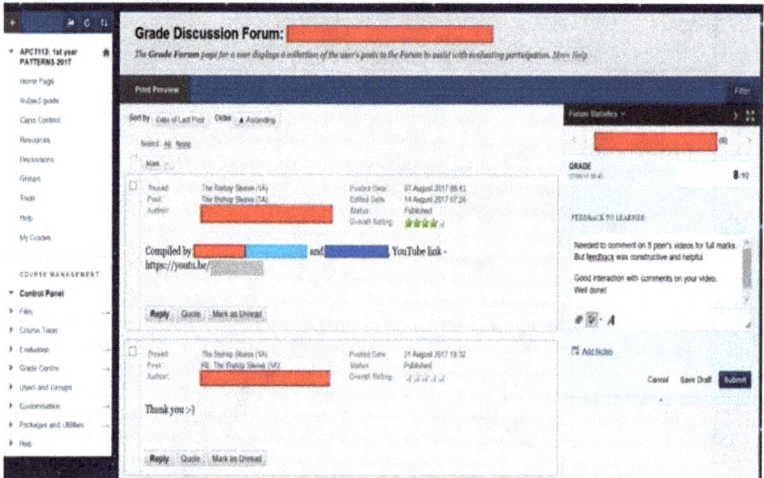

Screenshot from the online grading of discussion forum posts

Author Biography

Michaella Cavanagh is a passionate blended-learning enthusiast, who lectures in the Department of Fashion and Textiles at the Durban University of Technology in South Africa. She teaches Pattern Technology (pattern drafting) to first-year and Kaledo (a fashion specific computer-aided design software) to second-year students.

Michaella Cavanagh

An Authoring Tool for Teachers to Design and Create 3D Virtual Labs

Giannis Chantas[1], Dimitrios Ververidis[1], Panagiotis Migkotzidis[1], Eleftherios Anastasovitis[1], Anastasios Papazoglou-Chalikias[1], Efstathios Nikolaidis[1], Spiros Nikolopoulos[1], Ioannis Kompatsiaris[1], Georgios Mavromanolakis[2], Line Ebdrup Thomsen[3], Benedikte Mikkelsen[3], Anders Drachen[3], Antonios Liapis[4], Georgios N. Yannakakis[4], Marc Müller[5] and Fabian Hadiji[5]

[1]Centre of Research and Technology, Hellas, Greece
[2]Ellinogermaniki Agogi, Greece
[3]Aalborg University, Denmark
[4]University of Malta
[5]goedle.io Gmbh

Abstract: This work focuses on the design and implementation of a tool that allows educators to author 3D virtual labs. The methodology is based on web 3D frameworks such as three.js and WordPress that allow making simplified interfaces for modifying Unity3D templates. Two types of templates namely one for Chemistry and one for Wind Energy labs were developed that allow to test the generalization, user-friendliness and usefulness of such an approach. Results of testing the tool have shown that educators are much interested on the general concept, but several improvements should be made towards the user-friendliness and the intuitiveness of the interfaces in order to allow the inexperienced educators in 3D gaming to make such an attempt.

1. Introduction to initiative objectives

In this document, we present the e-Learning related objective and the work undertaken towards them in the context of the ENVISAGE[1] project. The work focuses on the development of an authoring tool that teachers and educators can use to build virtual labs with 3D graphics as interface, without the need to acquire programming expertise. Moreover, using this tool, we have created two types of virtual labs, that of chemistry and wind-

---

[1] http://www.envisage-h2020.eu/

energy (ENVISAGE, 2018a), which have also been tested by teachers and students. Lastly, another important feature of the created labs is the data analytics functionality, which is embedded automatically via the tool to the labs. With this functionality, we aim to help teachers to monitor the learning process of the students and modify the labs according to guidelines and the learning data analysis.

Video games that simulate real-life learning environments are used in a frequent basis by Educational organizations. These are environments design to train the learning in a controlled manner, they use mostly 3D graphics and, thus, they have been significantly improved in the last years with the advent of Virtual Reality (VR) technologies. There are several organizations that have put them in use in education and training (Bavelier, 2012), (Labster, 2018). However, several shortcomings, such as the high cost and the luck of proper design, hinder their expansion to education and other fields. With our work, we seek to provide technological solutions to the problem of overcoming these obstacles. More specifically, we provide a proper designed authoring tool that allows the creation of virtual labs with a small cost.

Indeed, it costs a lot in general to develop games (Lovato, 2015). The process of making a game mainly consists of the following phases: a) the design scenario, b) the design of the game-play and the game characteristics, c) the creation of the artistic content, d) the software development and finally e) the dissemination of the game to the gaming community and its promotion to the market. Educational organizations however cannot easily follow all these steps, since they lack in many of the above expert knowledge and experience. Therefore, there is a need to automate this process, at least the software development and content design phases. Thus, the main objective in our work is to replace the development and content creation phases with an automated one, which is based on game project templates that incorporate high level abstraction. More specifically, the templates allow the game designer and developer to create content in an abstract manner, exploiting the object behaviour inheritance of the templates. In this way, unnecessary details are hidden from the developers (i.e., teachers, in our work and evaluation procedure) by allowing items to inherit a predesigned structure. Furthermore, our methodology relies on the development of a user-friendly platform that is used to create and design virtual labs by using high quality game engines and web interfaces. More specifically, we employ WordPress (WordPress, 2017) web content management system in order to develop an editor for Unity3D game engine (Miles, 2016). This editor is actually a web portal for educators, allowing them to build educational games. To make a game, a game project must be first created, which provides to the teachers the ability to edit the game to be create. Then, the project game is compiled by the Unity3D game engine and the game output is therefore a game-like virtual lab.

Another novel and important aspect of our work is the incorporation of game analytics methodologies to the educational virtual labs borrowed from the data analytics technology (Drachen, 1989). Analytics are an essential part of improving general software products. In the developed templates and the authoring tool, analytics and visualizations were implemented, thus, inheriting data tracking and analytics visualizations to the games. This enables the educators using the virtual labs to receive feedback about the effectiveness of their labs and take decisions and make changes to the games accordingly.

2. Infrastructure
To achieve the above, the ENVISAGE consortium was designed accordingly: it consists of three research organizations, two of them being the universities of Malta and Aalborg, having great expertise in game analytics. The third is CERTH, with many years of experience in research projects and has the main role of the coordinator and integrating the developed technologies. Also, Ellinogermaniki-Agogi (EA) provides the E-Learning expertise and the educational facilities. Lastly, an SME, goedle.io, provides the expertise in tracking and maintaining play-through trajectories.

The software used to implement the infrastructure that is open consists of WordPress, the developed plug-in (Github, 2018), and Unity3D game engine. The aforementioned technologies are open and free to install. As regards the Analytics server, which is provided by GIO, it is a commercial system and it is not provided for free2. An instance of the server, having the role of the software infrastructure core and maintained by CERTH, is connected with the analytics server of GIO; it is accessible via the link: https://envisagelabs.iti.gr

---

[2] http://goedle.io

Regarding the testing and evaluation of the tool, EA has executed tests on the tool by organizing workshops at its premises, which emulate educational and learning contexts.

3. Challenges

The challenges at developing the authoring tool are mainly the design of an architecture that integrates all the analytics and game design modules and the development of a game creating tool that is user friendly and efficient. To overcome these challenges, the authoring tool developed in our work (ENVISAGE, 2018b), as its name suggest, supports the authoring of virtual labs through the usage of certain templates. At this point of development, we focused on two types of templates, namely the Chemistry and the Wind-Energy templates; in other words, two types of games can be created at this point by the tool, i.e., chemistry and wind energy virtual labs. In order to make a template, several steps must be followed. First, a prototype game is designed and it is implemented into Unity3D. Analytics tracking functions are also embedded during game implementation. In this way, any generated game has already the tracking functionality incorporated. Next, the YAML code of the prototype game is split into pieces of code that are inserted into WordPress data structures. In this way, the template is generated, which allows in essence the game refactoring through adjusting the parameters of the game that are adjustable through the authoring tool and the use of the template.

Then, the web front-end interface is built according to the requirements for modifications on the split code.
The game template can be adjusted by an educator using the front-end and compiled on the server side.

Adjusting the template parameters so as to produce a specific game is the core of the game authoring provided by our tool. A link of the game produced by the compilation is provided for downloading or accessing the game for WebGL versions. After a game has been deployed, any game data are sent to an analytics server that performs all the analysis. The game analytics are sent back to the authoring tool and are presented through proper visualizations to be inspected by the educator, in order the latter to make edits in the game accordingly.

The overall architecture of the authoring tool is shown in Figure 1. The backbone of the system is the Master Server, which contains the creation, editing and design functionalities. The Analytics Server, collects, stores, and process raw game data.

A usage scenario is the following. The educator access the platform front-end via a web browser. The front-end provides to the author the ability to edit the 3D scenes of the game, place the 3D objects (i.e., assets) and define the possible interactions between the player and the game. The platform makes available 3D assets of certain behavioural categories that the educator can easily use. The educator makes the necessary configurations and saves them into a new Game Project.

After configuring the Game Project, and setting up the scenes with the required assets, the educator defines the export format such as Windows, Mac, or WebGL in order for the game to be compiled and waits to receive the binary (Windows or Mac), or the link for WebGL compiled games. The educator provides the game to the learners for playing. When the game is played, it sends game data to the Analytics server. The data are aggregated and augmented with statistics and various features extracted with machine learning methodologies, which can be found in the technical reports (ENVISAGE, 2018d) and (ENVISAGE, 2018e). The analytics are served back to the Master server in order to be visualized.

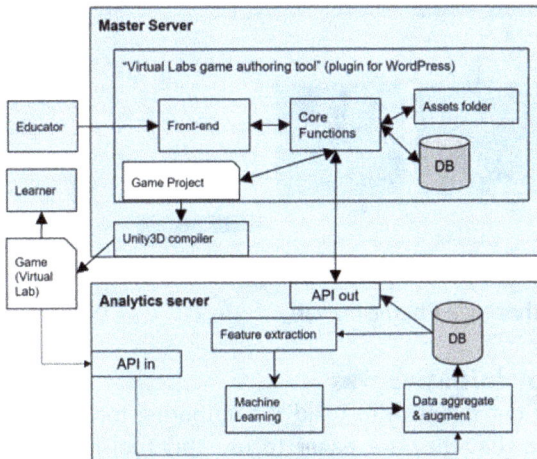

Figure 1: Overall architecture of the system.

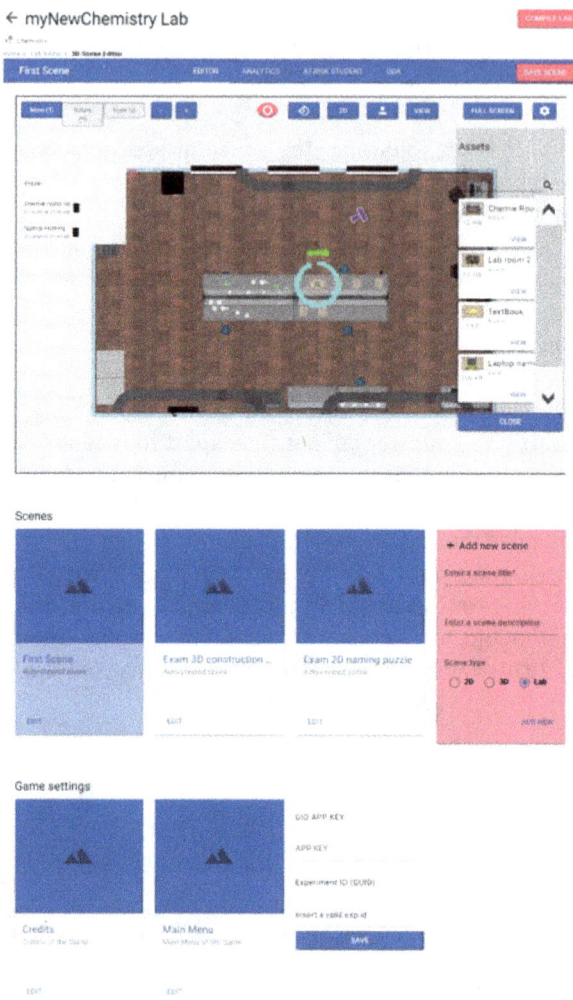

Figure 2: Authoring a Chemistry Lab

4. How our initiative was

The users of our initiative to build the authoring tool for creating virtual labs declared that they are eager to use this tool for their classes and found the software generally easy to use and useful. Next, we present the results of the evaluation of the authoring tool and the virtual labs created using it. Two methods are applied to evaluate the authoring tool: heuristic evaluation and user testing. Next, we describe both methods along with the evaluation results.

4.1 Heuristic Evaluation
Usability experts performed a heuristic evaluation on the authoring tool in terms of the user-friendliness of its user interface. They utilized the 10 usability heuristics originated by Jakob Nielsen (Nielsen, 1994). The evaluation focused on the functionalities of the authoring tool. The most common issues found during the analysis were related to missing previews, a lack of tool tips and help functions and inadequate descriptions of the authoring tool's functionalities. Such issues are natural to appear at this point of development. Many of the issues are related to missing content or ambiguous terminology and will hence not require a substantial amount of recourses to correct. In a future development cycle, we went through these issues renamed the functionalities, changed the design and add more tool tips where it is needed.

4.2 User test of authoring tool
Questionnaires were used to collect the feedback from the test participants for evaluating the authoring tool, with questions based on (Davis, 1989). In the questionnaires, the teachers were asked to give a score to statements with rating options ranging from "unlikely (1) to "likely" (7) and "strongly disagree" to "strongly agree". For the tests, the test participants were given a set of authoring tasks for creating labs, e.g., adding 3D objects and placing them. There were 5 test participants all of whom were teachers.

The questions related to the usefulness of the tool show that most teachers have a positive attitude. While there were quite a few comments that remarked negatively on the tools user-friendliness in the tested iteration there were also several comments that expressed a confidence that the authoring tool could offer benefits for the teachers going forward once more iterations are completed.

What the answers reveal during the evaluation is that the test participants encountered difficulties working with the authoring tool but at the same time they expressed an interest in the tool going forward and enjoyed the possibility being able to create a 3D experience for their classroom. The most negative comments regard to the user-friendliness of the tool. Suggestions such as adding tool-tips, more feedback from the system, simpler help functionality, as well as an undo function could greatly improve some of the issues and should be considered in future developments. This enabled us to redesign the tool by taking into account the comments and suggestions, leading in this way in a more user friendly interface and engaging authoring experience.

4.3 Virtual labs and learning content

To evaluate the type of virtual labs and learning content that can be created using the authoring tool the teachers were asked to assess a demo version of such a lab, i.e., the Wind Energy Lab (ENVISAGE, 2018a). The test participants evaluating the virtual lab were the same as for the user test for the authoring tool, see Section 4.2. They were given a questionnaire and asked to consider how much they (dis)agreed with statements regarding the students' engagement with the lab, quality of educational contents, the fit in terms of the students' abilities, and the teachers' expectations.

Regarding the quality of the learning content, the teachers agreed that the virtual labs can be integrated into a learning context. The interface however was rated as "needs improvement", thus, we have improved it dramatically since then. The statements relating to the students' engagement and enjoyment of the virtual lab are concentrated on the neutral midpoint. Though the teachers were satisfied with the content, they proposed to further develop the content of the labs so as to better support their teaching.

4.4 Game analytics

Game analytics is something that educators are not familiar with, and therefore we have conducted an evaluation procedure in order to find which types of game analytics visualizations would be useful to them. The visualizations shown to the participants were a dashboard, bar charts, force-directed graphs, chord diagrams and an absolute time-line. For evaluating the visualizations, the test participants were given a questionnaire with three metrics, each being visualized in two to three different ways. In Figure 3, a game analytics dashboard example is depicted. Participants were asked to rank the visualizations internally with the metric and in relation to, e.g., best overview and most informative. The participants were also encouraged to add more in-depth descriptions of why they had ranked the visualizations in the order they did. This evaluation therefore helped us narrow down which visualization is more useful.

Most of the testers had experience in reading and extracting the information from a visualization, which helped understanding them better. This shows that presenting data analytics and conveying information efficiently depends also on the receiver information interpretational prowess. This also explains that simpler visualizations were more understandable than complex ones. More details can be found in the respective technical report (ENVISAGE, 2018f).

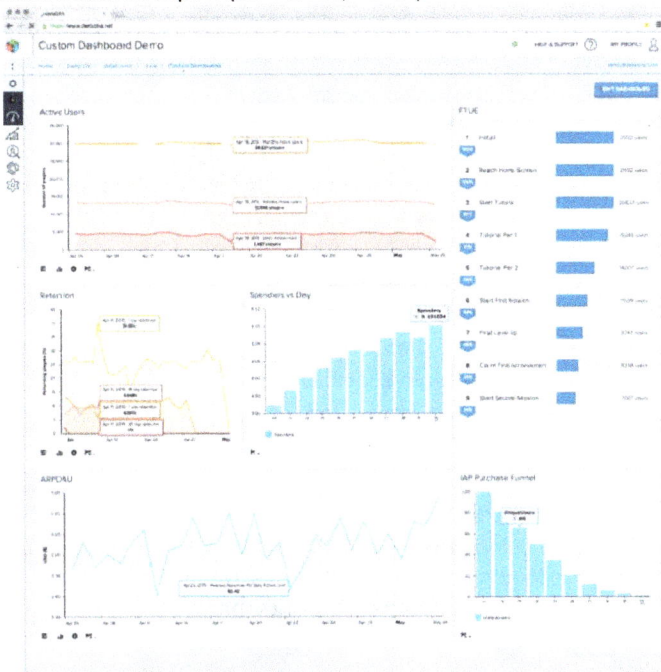

Figure 3: Visualizations of a dashboard

5. The learning outcomes

In general, the authoring tool that we presented has been proven to be an engaging and attractive to teachers and students as a solution for authoring Wind Energy and Chemistry labs (ENVISAGE, 2018c). Moreover, it was shown that analytics is feasible to be embedded automatically in a lab, and their use is understandable and meaningful. However, the usage of the tool by inexperienced users was proven to be a challenge. We saw by the answers to the questionnaires that the tool was accepted by the educational experts as a potential tool to be used in the class on the condition of several improvements in its user friendliness. Thus, we can conclude that the authoring tool architecture by the combination of the web based authoring capabilities was proven successful, but more have to be done in order to be used in a realistic educational context.

Finally, the students evaluated our initiative positively, they show that they find this learning process more engaging and entertaining, and they believe that they can motivate students learn about specific fields, as an addition to the standard methods of learning.

6. Plans to further develop the initiative

In the future, we aim to include more data analytics and visualizations in other large scale context, i.e., many schools, even belonging in different countries. Also, increasing the user-friendliness of the user interface is also a part of our future work since by doing this we believe more educators will be convinced to use our product.

Another aspect of our work that we plan to further develop in the future is that of learning analytics. More specifically, we plan to expand the types of data being tracked by the users and employ more complex machine learning algorithms. Devising novel algorithms can also be an option.

Lastly, we believe it is worth to expand the abilities of the authoring tool so as to be able to develop virtual labs related to extra scientific (or artistic) fields. We plan to develop new virtual lab templates for our tool for scientific fields like physics, maths, linguistics, music, etc.

References

Bavelier, D. 2012, Your brain in video games [Online]. Available from: https://www.ted.com/talks/daphne_bavelier_your_brain_on_video_games/transcript?language=en
Davis, F. D. 1989, 'Perceived usefulness, perceived ease of use, and user acceptance of information technology', MIS Quarterly, vol. 13, No. 3 (Sep., 1989), pp. 319-340.
Drachen, A., Canossa, A. 2016, Game analytics, Springer (2016).
ENVISAGE 2018a, Unity WebGL Player | Wind Farm Simulator [Online]. Available from: http://www.envisage-h2020.eu/games/energy/v1_1_3/ [2 Oct. 2018].

ENVISAGE 2018b, Final version of the "Virtual labs authoring tool". Available from: http://www.envisage-h2020.eu/wp-content/uploads/2018/05/D4.4_FinalVersionVirtualLabsAuthoringTool_Final.pdf, project deliverable, on-line since 2018.

ENVISAGE 2018c, 'Implementation of the educational scenarios and evaluation report', [Online]. Available from: http://www.envisage-h2020.eu/wp-content/uploads/2017/10/D5.2-Implementation-of-the-educational-scenarios-and-evaluation-report_Final-version_V3.pdf, project deliverable, on-line 2018

ENVISAGE 2018d, Preliminary predictive analytics and course adaptation methods [Online]. Available from: http://www.envisage-h2020.eu/wp-content/uploads/2017/12/D3.1.pdf, project deliverable, on-line 2018.

ENVISAGE 2018e, User profiling and behavioral modeling based on shallow analytics, [Online]. Available from: http://www.envisage-h2020.eu/wp-content/uploads/2017/09/D2.2Final.pdf, project deliverable, on-line 2018.

ENVISAGE 2018f, Visualization strategies for course progress reports [Online], http://www.envisage-h2020.eu/wp-content/uploads/2017/07/D2.3-Visualization-strategies-for-course-progress-reports.pdf, project deliverable, on-line 2018.

Github 2018, WordPressUnity3DEditor plugin for WordPress [Online], Available from: https://github.com/Envisage-H2020/Virtual-labs-authoring-tool, 2018.

Labster 2018, Empower and engage your STEM students [Online], Available form: https://www.labster.com

Lovato, N. 2015, 'What is the budget breakdown of AAA games?' [Online], Available from: https://www.quora.com/What-is-the-budget-breakdown-of-AAA-games

Miles, J. 2016, 'Unity 3D and PlayMaker Essentials: Game Development from Concept to Publishing', AK Peters/CRC Press (2016).

Nielsen, J. 1994, 'Usability engineering', Elsevier (1994).

Wordpress Wikipedia 2018, Wikipedia's official web-page for WordPress [Online]. Available from: https://en.wikipedia.org/wiki/WordPress.

Contributing Author biographies

Dr. Giannis Chantas has been with ITI-CERTH for the last five years as a postdoctoral research fellow. He has participated in a number of FP7, HORIZON2020 and national research projects. His research interests include Bayesian inference, image and video processing, stochastic models and methods for machine learning.

Dr. Dimitrios Ververidis is a Web, Android, and Unity3D developer interested for Educational and Cultural applications. He interested in improving classrooms and cultural facilities with innovative technologies that allow for the education of the future. Such technologies include Augmented - Virtual Reality, Games, Internet of Things, and mobile solutions.

Giannis Chantas et al

Panagiotis Migkotzidis graduated from Computer science department of university of Ioannina in 2017. The same year he started working as a research assistant in the Center of Research and Technology Hellas (CERTH). His main research interests are serious games and interactive media.

Anastasios Papazoglou - Chalikias is a researcher and developer in CERTH - ITI with a focus on UX/UI design and web development. He participated in many FP7 and HORIZON2020 projects such as Live+Gov, iTreasures, MAMEM & ENVISAGE.

Efstathios Nikolaidis is a research assistant in the Centre for Research and Technology Hellas since July 2015. He graduated as IT Engineer at Dpt. of Informatics of Technological Educational Institute of Thessaloniki in 2011. He's also received a MSc degree in Computer Systems at University of Macedonia (Dpt. Applied Informatics)

Eleftherios Anastasovitis received his Computer Science degree in 2005. In 2014 he received his M.Sc in Cultural Informatics and Communication. In 2017, Eleftherios received his M.Ed in Adult Education from the Hellenic Open University. He is PhD candidate in Applied Informatics. He is currently a research assistant in ITI/CERTH.

Dr. Spiros Nikolopoulos (M) is currently a post-doctoral research fellow at the Centre for Research & Technology Hellas. His research interests include image analysis, indexing and retrieval, multimodal analysis, multimedia analysis using semantic information and integration of context and content for multimedia interpretation.

Dr. Ioannis Kompatsiaris is a Researcher Director at CERTH-ITI. His research interests include multimedia, big data and social media analytics, semantics, eHealth, security and culture applications. He is the co-author of 129 papers in journals and more than 420 papers in international conferences. He is an IEEE Senior Member.

Dr. Georgios Mavromanolakis works at the Research and Development Department of Ellinogermaniki Agogi/Greece as senior researcher and project manager of EU funded projects on science, technology and education. He has coordinated at European and national level the

48

implementation of various projects, among others, Pathway, GoLab, Ark of Inquiry, Icaros.

Line Ebdrup Thomsen holds a M.Sc. in Information Studies from AAU and has previously worked as an IT-consultant and User Researcher. Her research has primarily been focused on the design and evaluation of games and she has presented her work on multiple international conferences.

Benedikte Mikkelsen holds a Master in Game Design and Media Technology from ITU. Since graduation she has worked in both academia and the industry, focusing on data analysis and developing games for impact. Among her clients are The Danish Ministry of Health, The Danish Military and a range of NGOs.

Anders Drachen is a Professor at the DC Labs, University of York and a veteran Data Scientist. His work in data and game science is focused on game analytics and games user research. He is one of the most published scientists worldwide on these topics, having authored over 100 publications.

Antonios Liapis is a Lecturer at the Institute of Digital Games, University of Malta, conducting research in artificially intelligent design tools and computational blending of semantics, visuals, audio, plot and levels. Antonios has worked on 6 EU-funded projects, has published over 70 academic papers and has received several awards.

Georgios N. Yannakakis is a Professor and Director of the Institute of Digital Games, University of Malta, a game AI expert that has published over 220 papers in machine learning, affective computing and computational creativity. His work has been cited broadly and has received multiple awards from prestigious venues.

Marc Muller, prior to co-founding goedle.io, has worked at the Fraunhofer IAIS, in Germany. His research focused on artificial intelligence. He holds an M.Sc in Computer Sciences and has published and presented his work at multiple international conferences. Since 2015, he works in the field of user behavior prediction.

Fabian Hadiji is CEO and Co-Founder at goedle.io. He holds a PhD in AI from TU Dortmund University and he has more than ten years of experience in machine learning research and applications. He is a Fraunhofer Alumni and used to work as Data Scientist at GameAnalytics.

Bothersome Beasties (and how to deal with them!)

Samantha Clarke, Sylvester Arnab and Lauren Heywood
Disruptive Media Learning Lab, Coventry University
ab4588@coventry.ac.uk
aa8110@coventry.ac.uk
ac0146@coventry.ac.uk

1. Introduction

The practice of self-reflection for some students is often thought of as tedious and more often than not, even though the benefits of self-reflection have long been documented (Dewey, 1997; Jarvis, 1992; Nesbit, 2012), little time is given (to the fault of both students and educators) to building upon the necessary skills required for aiding this process (Hussein, 2006). An issue commonly reported in regards to self-reflection development in learners, is the lack of knowledge or time to achieve reflection in terms of Dewey's set out definition; that it should be active and persistent (Quinton and Smallbone, 2010). If a learner exhibits reflective practice, all too often it is not a consistent custom in which the learner leads the exercise. There is a need to ensure that reflection is built into the learning materials in a way that makes it a crucial element to the learning process, and in short that the learners accept that it is a valuable component of their learning. In light of the theory and their own practice observations, the creators were therefore keen to explore methods that could make the process of self-reflection more appealing and that could be built into a module from a position of a primary functional role, rather than a secondary afterthought. It was essential that whatever was developed, would fit easily and be relevant to their teaching within a University setting.

Another core consideration was the need to develop a tool that helped support the use of flexible and timely formative feedback from lecturer to student. One of the biggest issues at the moment in education is that results take too long to get back to the students and are completely impersonal, making that kind of feedback essentially irrelevant. In short, feedback needs to be personal, and it needs to be fast. To that end, educators are beginning to refocus their attention on relevant, practical formative feedback for students during lessons or very soon after, rather than relying only on summative assessments. The goal of formative feedback is to monitor student learning as they progress through the lifecycle of an activity in order to provide ongoing feedback that can be used by instructors to improve their teaching and by students to improve their learning. More specifically, formative feedback helps students identify their strengths and weaknesses and target areas that need work. Having this open/ real time level of communication that students could use to actively assess their own working practice is considered to be a best practice approach to supporting student development. If a learner exhibits reflective practice, all too often it is not a consistent custom in which the learner leads the exercise. There is a need to ensure that reflection is built into the learning materials in a way that makes it a crucial element to the learning process, and in short that the learners accept that it is a valuable component of their learning. It is also argued that students must take more responsibility and empower learners through the use of self-directed learning. Giroux et al (1989) argues:

"We have to see classroom not only as an arena of indoctrination and enforcing submission into the dominant beliefs and ideologies, but also as ' a cultural terrain that promotes learner empowerment and self-transformation". (Giroux et al, 1989)

Building on the ideals of formative feedback principles, we were also keen to explore the space of peer formative feedback, allowing student peers to share their own insights and knowledge, and to also feel like they were contributing to the development of others as an altruistic way of working alongside each other.

2. The infrastructure

The self-reflection website titled 'Bothersome Beasties (and how to deal with them!)' was developed from a piece of action-based participatory research that was conducted within a 11-week, Design Thinking Module for Second Year Undergraduate students at Coventry University, UK. Based on a gamification approach to learning and inspired by Dungeons and

Dragons (D&D), a table-top roleplaying games system developed by Gygax and Arneson (1974), the initial research trialed a host of game mechanics such as, but not limited to: character creation, customisation, skills development, leveling over time, story-telling and a game-masters feedback in order to get students developing self-reflection skills and how to think creatively about how they build and learn from their experiences in the classroom.

Using the Disruptive Media Learning Lab's, GameChangers: 'Remixing Play into a Gameplan' (GameChangers, 2016) open course workshop, the authors set about developing the main principles of D&D into a system that could be used to help facilitate student self-reflection in an interesting and entertaining way.

The design of the tool started out with an inspection of the mechanics of D&D and a planning session of how it was to work in a University module setting. Character development via character sheets, character attributes, enemies and team-based role-play/narrative were some of the main factors that make up the game of D&D. Initially, the students were required to reflect on various areas as described below:

Monsters: Students will be asked to identify at least one problem concerned with the ongoing module work (this could be a personal development, team or project related problem) and they must pose a solution in order to defeat said monster.

Example: A student's team has a problem with deciding on a particular issue to address with their project. Their monster is the 'sludge of indecision'. The student then suggests that in order to overcome this monster, the team must meet on another day and make a firm decision on which issue they are going to concentrate on.

Allies: Students will be asked to identify at least one person/ type of person/ company/ Contact that may be useful to help their research and development of their final concept/product.

Example: A team proposes targeting a solution for raising awareness in student mental health. Each member of the team proposes a contact to talk to for research purposes, this could be for example a staff member from the Wellness Centre.

Treasures: Students will be asked to identify at least one resource that they may need to help the research, design and/or development of their concept/ product. Students will also be asked to identify how they will go about obtaining the resource.

Example: A student identifies that for their board game concept, the team would like some physical pieces for their prototype. The student then suggests they look at the 3D printing resources available at the University.

This reflection part of the research of using D&D to gamify a course was found to be the most popular amongst students. A mid-way pilot evaluation indicated these results in that the students found the area of the gamification approach to be most useful and fun; the re-framing of issues/ problems into 'beasts or monsters' that was inspired by the idea of a 'Monster Manual' used in D&D. Inspired by the findings of the focus group interviews, the 'Bothersome Beasties' website was created for students to use as a method of identifying, re-framing and suggesting solutions to resolve issues they were having.

The tool is a free, open source, customised WordPress website (hosted by Domains Coventry https://dmll.org.uk/tool/coventry-domains/) that students can use anonymously (or use their names), to document any issues they are having that is affecting their educational journey. The tool is available online and does not require a log in or a download which allows for the tool to be accessed anytime/ anywhere with no limitations. The compendium further acts as a guide in which students from across any number of modules can view other student's issues and comment on them in a helpful way.

The Core features of the website:

2.1 Overview of all 'Beasties'

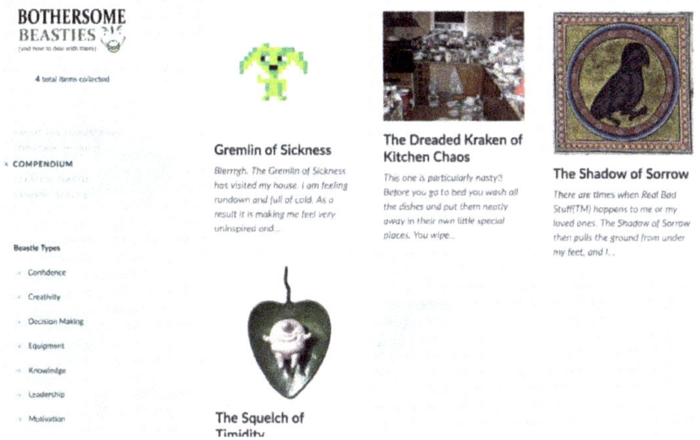

Figure 1: Front page overview of all 'Beasties'

This front-page lists all of the beasties that have been added. Students and lecturers can go through them to browse or pick out interesting problems that may be relevant to them.

2.2 Handy Overview of Theory Behind Tool

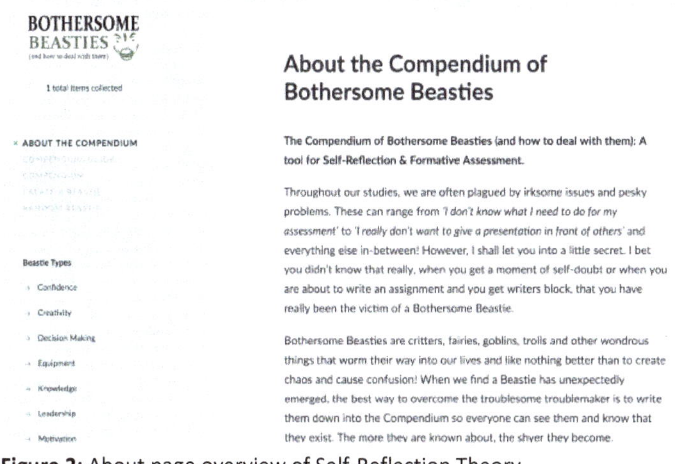

Figure 2: About page overview of Self-Reflection Theory

Included in the website is a section that explains the theory behind why self-reflection is an important tool for students to gain skills on.

2.3 Simple Form to 'Create a new Beastie'

BEASTIES
(and how to deal with them)

4 total items collected

FIND THE COMPENDIUM
COMPENDIUM FIND
COMPENDIUM
× CREATE A BEASTIE
RANDOM BEASTIE

Beastie Types
→ Confidence
→ Creativity
→ Decision Making
→ Equipment
→ Knowledge
→ Leadership
→ Motivation
→ Multidisciplinary

Create a New Beastie

Got a Beastie that is troubling you? Whether it is a Disruptive Demon or Troublesome Troll, record it here so that it appears in the Compendium for all to see!

ⓘ Need to add a Beastie to the Compendium? Yes! Use the form below to share it. Fields marked * are required.

Beastie Name *
Enter a unique and interesting name for your Beastie. Example: The Slug of Sleepiness!

Upload an Image of your Beastie *
Upload an image by dragging its icon to the window that opens when clicking "Select Image" button. Larger JPG, PNG images are best. To preserve animation, GIFs should be no larger than 500px wide.

Select Image

Figure 3: Form to Create a New 'Beastie'

→ Create Your Own

Search Form

Tags
DMLL 2018

A SPLOT on the Web: Twitter know
Beasties.
Beast slogging
Based on FutureLearn theme by
Anders Norén.
(1)

Character Name
Take credit for sharing this item by entering your character name.

Anonymous

Describe your Beastie *
Enter a reflective description of your Beastie. Tell us the problem and why is it affecting you?

Visual   Text

Paragraph   ▾   **B**   *I*   ≔   ≣   **"**   ≣   ≣   ≣   ⸖   🔗   ☒   ↺   ✕   ▦

Figure 4: Continued Form to Create a New Beastie

Easy to follow form for students to fill out in order to post a 'beastie to the compendium. The form consists of a 'Beastie name', 'Image of beastie', 'name of person uploading', 'description of beastie', 'beastie type', 'tag

56

your beastie', 'contact the curator' sections, and has been condensed to ensure students don't feel it is too much effort to fill out.

2.4 Beastie Types Section

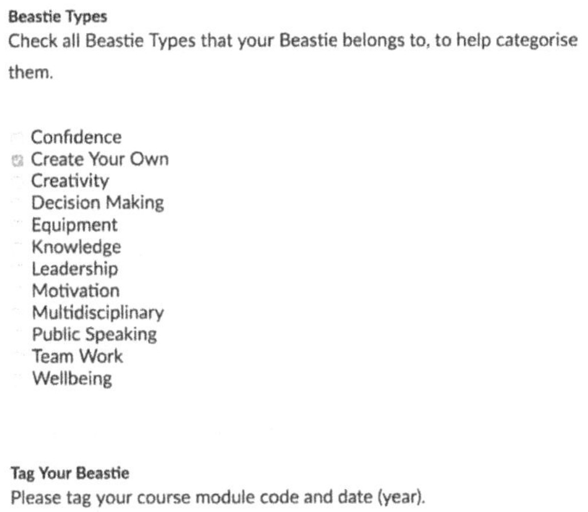

Beastie Types
Check all Beastie Types that your Beastie belongs to, to help categorise
them.

- Confidence
- ☑ Create Your Own
- Creativity
- Decision Making
- Equipment
- Knowledge
- Leadership
- Motivation
- Multidisciplinary
- Public Speaking
- Team Work
- Wellbeing

Tag Your Beastie
Please tag your course module code and date (year).

Figure 5: Area to Select Category of Beastie

In order to identify and to help student find other issues in the same areas, a 'beastie type' section has been added so that students can identify what type of problem it is that they are dealing with. Students can then click on one of the types on the main page and it will bring up all of the issues under that heading, allowing them to read through specific issues that may be relevant to them. Helping students to identify their issues, also allows lecturers/ facilitators to offer specific advice.

2.5 Tags

Tags

DMLL 2018

A SPLOT on the Web: Bothersome
Beasties.
Blame cogdog.
Based on Fukasawa theme by

Figure 6: Tags for Easy Tracking of Beasts in the Website

Students can tag their beasties, which allows lectures to keep track of all the beasties associated with a specific module/ course/ year or a mixture of all three. The tags appear on the front page of the website, that lecturers can look for their course to just bring up their student's beasties. This allows use of the website across as many as needed courses and institutions.

2.6 Contact the Curators

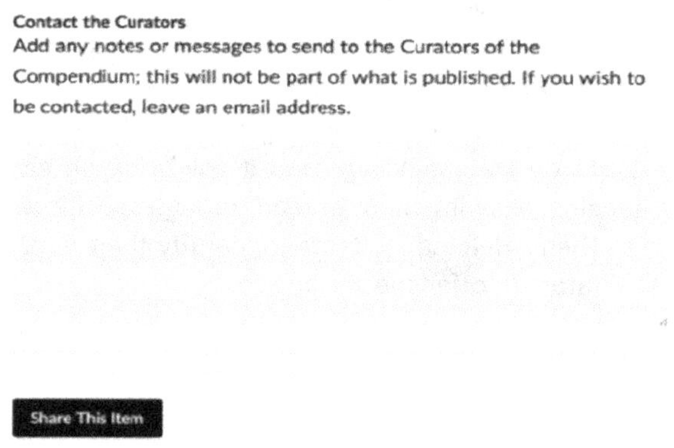

Contact the Curators
Add any notes or messages to send to the Curators of the
Compendium; this will not be part of what is published. If you wish to
be contacted, leave an email address.

Share This Item

Figure 7: Contact a Lecturer Form

The website allows students to ask to contact the curators directly for advice. This is really useful if a student has a problem that they believe needs immediate attention, and is helpful for the lecturers to keep on top of connecting with their students. Because of the anonymous nature of the website, it can also be a good way for students to share more personal issues with lecturers who may have problems coming forward face to face/ being known.

2.7 Direct Formative Feedback Mechanism

1 Comment

collector
MARCH 29, 2018

Dear Zygmunt Von Noobzen,

The curators thoroughly sympathise. This is perhaps one of the hardest to conquer Beasties. Popping up unexpectedly and without warning and for others it has been with them a long time. When you are feeling plagued by the Shadow of Sorrow, it is very hard to be motivated with being productive. But as you have reflected, this particular Beastie does have a weakness. Support. And thats what we are here to do. Perhaps others will share tales of how they have conquered this Beastie in time, but for now, know that there is always a helping hand at the other end of a keyboard. Know that it is not weakness to ask for help, in fact, we believe it shows strength. We curators love helping and if there is any a time you need to banish this Beastie, know you can turn to us. We can provide links to direct services or simply an ear.

REPLY   EDIT

Figure 8: Anonymous Commenting on the Site

After a student, has posted, a lecturer can go and post underneath the 'beastie' offering advice and feedback where needed. In the example, above (which was a real student) the lecturers suggest the student contact them if needed as they have links to services or support that can help in the area they wrote about. As it is an open forum, other students and lecturers can post to offer advice and support as well, encouraging the use of peer feedback and support. The comments are moderated.

3. The challenges

As the 'Bothersome Beasties' website was developed from a participatory action-research approach, the main challenges/ issues were addressed in this new iteration of the 'beastie' website reflection tool. The original method of reframing problems into monsters was delivered via a paper-based version, where students would physically collect a monster that represented an issue to them that week, and they would put it into a physical journal and reflect on it.

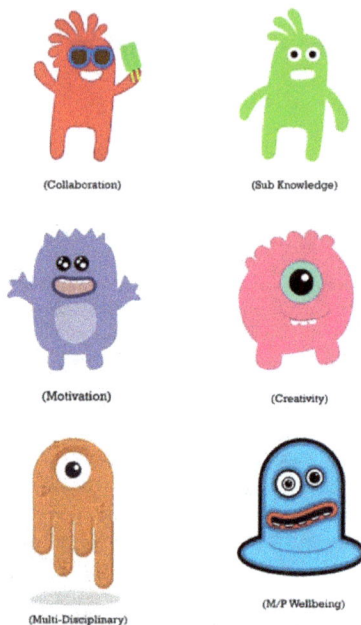

(Collaboration)

(Sub Knowledge)

(Motivation)

(Creativity)

(Multi-Disciplinary)

(M/P Wellbeing)

Figure 9: Original Paper-Based 'Beasties'

The student feedback that was gathered from this first paper-based approach to delivery included:

- "We could edit points through a digital system that would be easier to manage".
- "Instead of a physical journal and monsters to reflect, an electronic version would be better. To do it in class."
- "Managing the monsters online would be so much easier as I lose the paper bits sometimes."
- "I feel like there are not enough options with the monsters. Sometimes I have different issues."

In response to this, we created the 'Bothersome Beasties' website to address the student's issues of management and accessibility, and provided a system with more varied monster types including a 'create your own' setting. So far, due to the fact that the application is completely open and anyone can access it from any point, there have been no technical issues involved with the use of the website. Equally, at the present moment we have encountered no other challenges with this approach.

4. How the initiative was received

A second semi-structured focus group questionnaire was used to gather feedback on the updated 'Bothersome Beasties. The following is a sample of the feedback that was gathered.

- Well, I think it's quite better than the actual paper monsters. Supports creativity of a person more. Plus, when its anonymous, they can always say their real problems without being worried.
- I think it makes the process easier and makes you want to use it a bit more.
- It's quite creative and good to have a clear vision on your problems. Creating a monster that represents your problems might give you an idea for a solution.
- I think it gives you, it might make you feel insecure but if it's a monster it might make you feel better/ easier in tackling it.
- Yeah, I'd use it again – because it would give me a clear vision, when I can see them I can see more clearly.
- More like with paper base you have to choose and more effort. Now its online it's a lot easier to access.
- I think it's really useful. Online is more that you can create your own issue. Sometimes you might not have an issue that falls into one of the categories, but this gives you options.
- The module has helped me to reflect on attributes. I used to do self-reflection on my entire session, but this has allowed me to reflect on individual attributes.
- In my team, I felt like I wasn't making much impact in my team, as I wasn't confident. I chose the monster confidence which helped me to reflect to be more outspoken about my ideas.
- I think it was good because if at the end of session there wasn't something up to scratch, you could choose the monster and talk about it. Something to reflect on.

- Found it awesome. It was really good and I enjoyed it. Really good idea.
- Found it quite interesting as someone who uses a journal myself – really awesome that the monsters are something to reflect on during the day and come back to.
- It helped people understand where they were going in the module.
- Really influenced way of thinking for sure. My way of seeing my mistakes.
- I can't find any negatives with the monsters.
- I think it was a positive experience and helped to understand the experience of the modules journey. Was useful to help write up at the end.
- Good thing was helped you to understand where you were going and helped to document ideas.

With the new iteration of the website, the 28 students that were interviewed all had positive things to say about the new format and the idea of using monsters as a reflection exercise. Although students posed some suggestions of further developing the tool, such as to include even more options for types of beasties, not one student had a negative comment on the use of the tool. Ongoing work with larger cohorts of students is currently underway for more insights.

5. The learning outcomes

The students who helped build and trialed this tool, were given a final assessment piece at the end of the 11-week course. The assessment was 1000-word essay that was a reflection piece on the development of their practical project work over the course of the module. As evidenced above in the findings gathered from the students, a lot of students used this tool to help them build their case for their assessment. Preliminary results also showed that this first group to use the tool, showed a better understanding and awareness of the reflection process over the previous cohort of students on the Design Thinking Module. Statistically, the second cohort who had access to the tool showed a grade average of 67.3809 against cohort A who did not have access to the tool that average was measured at 61.5862, showing an increase on reflection grades. Another examiner was used to ensure no bias in grade marking.

Based on the feedback gathered from the students, one of the most import findings in support of the use of this tool for future self-reflection exercises is that the students commented on how interesting, different and fun it had been. These are descriptions that are not usually associated with self-reflection exercises, and give hope for a different approach to developing these skills. The students also commented on how they would reflect on these monsters at the end of the day, or use them as a 'useful' guidance to form their thoughts and reflect on what happened in the lesson. Anything that encourages students to be more pro-active and take a self-directed approach to learning and development is a valuable learning outcome for more core learning skills development.

6. Plans to further develop the initiative

Following on from the initial trials of the website, the next stage of trials are currently running with Coventry University, Salford University (Media City) and The University of South Wales, Cardiff. The creators are running a large-scale trial with both students and lecturers to find out their opinions and feedback to further test the usefulness and acceptability of the tool to support self-reflect skills development.

Further feedback, suggestions and expert input will be sought to refine the tool further and reader feedback is welcomed. As the tool is an open-source resource, others are encouraged to use the website for their own needs.

A support system has been set up at Coventry University to help others to use this tool and adapt it for their own purposes. As the tool is also non-specific in terms of audience, the tool can be used in any branch of educational environment, whether that be high school, FE, University or adult education and is currently being pushed out as an example to other institutions to take up and use. Furthermore, the tool is also being developed as a case study of best-practice in teaching and learning for the use of all Coventry University members of staff.

As the tool is not-for-profit, the creators want to build up a support structure within the open education forum in which everyone has access to this best-practice tool that can be used to enhance their teaching and learning delivery and development. As such, we will work closely with this community of open education practitioners to develop the tool to suitable fit within this space, using Creative Commons licensing as a way to give back to the educational community.

References

Credit Continue. 2018. The Compendium of Bothersome Beasties (and how to deal with them!) [online]. Available from:
https://seriousgameslife.wordpress.com/2018/03/26/the-compendium-of-bothersome-beasties-a-splot-for-self-reflection-formative-feedback/ Accessed: [10th May 2018]

Dewey, J., 1997. How we think. Courier Corporation.

GameChangers., 2016. Remixing Play into a Gameplan. [online] Available from:
http://gamify.org.uk/workshop-remixing-play-into-a-gameplan/ Accessed: [29th April 2018]

Giroux, H. A., McLaren, P. L., & McLaren, P. (Eds.). (1989). Critical pedagogy, the state, and cultural struggle. Suny Press.

Gygax, G. and Arneson, D., 1974. Dungeons and dragons (Vol. 19). Lake Geneva, WI: Tactical Studies Rules.

Jarvis, P., 1992. Reflective practice and nursing. Nurse Education Today, 12(3), pp.174-181.

Hussein, J.W., 2006. Which One Is Better: Saying Student Teachers Don't Reflect or Systematically Unlocking Their Reflective Potentials: A Positive Experience from a Poor Teacher Education Faculty in Ethiopia. Australian Journal of Teacher Education, 31(2), p.1.

Nesbit, P.L., 2012. The role of self-reflection, emotional management of feedback, and self-regulation processes in self-directed leadership development. Human Resource Development Review, 11(2), pp.203-226.

Quinton, S. and Smallbone, T., 2010. Feeding forward: using feedback to promote student reflection and learning–a teaching model. Innovations in Education and Teaching International, 47(1), pp.125-135.

Contributing Author Biographies

Samantha Clarke is a practical developer and researcher of game-based learning and gamification applications primarily focused on the role of games and play in the educational environment. Her research and practice interests are mainly in the area of curiosity, narrative and puzzle led games that include escape rooms, D&D, mystery boxes and choose your own adventure style games. She has worked as a researcher and designer for several European and UK national projects which have focused on developing and delivering teaching and learning content via both analogue and digital game-based learning approaches for a range of formal and informal settings.

Sylvester Arnab leads research and applied innovation at the DMLL and he seeks to explore and exploit opportunities for external collaborations informed by the infusion of innovative practices within the DMLL and applied across the University and beyond. As a Professor of Games Science, he forefronts the investigation into the application of playful and gameful approaches in teaching and learning practices at the University, which include game-based learning, serious games, gamification and playful learning. He co-founded the GameChangers – a Game Design Thinking initiative, which is currently being adopted and adapted in other countries, such as Malaysia. The circle of impact of current and previous work framed under the playful and gameful learning has expanded beyond the University Group into national and international domains and sectors.

Lauren Heywood drives the adoption of new practices at Coventry University, supporting educators to rethink traditional approaches to teaching and learning. Much of Lauren's work with the Lab has focused around the application of open technologies to support interdisciplinary learning, digital making, and the development of student and staff digital fluency. This includes Coventry University's Domain of One's Own initiative Coventry. Domains, the DMLL's development of the use of Open Badges, and Mission Shakespeare, as well as a number of open tools that promote the inclusion of creative thinking and making as essential in generating rich educational experiences.

Naked and Exposed! Using Digistories to Unveil the Hidden Research Process

Laura Delgaty
Newcastle University, Newcastle Upon Tyne, UK
l.e.delgaty@ncl.ac.uk

Abstract:
Students undertaking educational research for the first time often encounter difficulties with the complexities of qualitative approaches, especially as it relates to the research process and related philosophies. The Masters of Medical Education programme at Newcastle University provides the opportunity for students to design and deliver a small-scale qualitative research project. This, often independent, undertaking is difficult. However, once completed, students should be competent in conducting basic research. It is relatively easy for students to conceptualise the end product as there are past examples of dissertations to view. However, what students traditionally struggle with, and academics find difficult to articulate, is the overall hidden research process which is far less visible. Along the research journey, our students, like others on similar programmes, submit small pieces of work as milestones of progress, and academics provide feedback on this work. Although this work is all held electronically on school servers, our current students only have access to select parts of this past work and there is no narrative or cohesion. As a result, a significant barrier to success, and therefore the problem for students, is the conceptualisation of the research process. Therefore, in an effort to make the tacit research process explicit, research digistories (RDS) as online educational resources were created for current students. They are organised, step-by-step illustrative cases, using past student milestones submitted with academic feedback already given, along with a central narrative. These multimedia stories were created using existing, archived materials. Development of the final template for the RDS required numerous drafts and three iterative focus groups. Although this final template was produced by the academic, it is in a format that can be populated easily and the RDS are now being created by an administrator. Both quantitative (web analytics) and qualitative data have been collected to evidence the impact on different stakeholders: current and past students, supervisors and the institution. The results are overwhelmingly positive. This teaching innovation responds to student need, a gap in current published practice and academic pressures. It is editable and can now be fully created by administrators, saving valuable academic time. Most importantly, there is evidence

this transferable and sustainable approach is helping academics unveil, and students make sense of, the hidden research process.

1. Introduction to Innovation

If story telling is central to human meaning, why, in the research world, is there not more story telling? (p. 505, Lewis 2011)

1.1 Background

Like many MScs, in the Masters of Medical Education programme at Newcastle University, students are expected to design and deliver a small scale educational and qualitative research project. Although the jump to autonomous research can be difficult (Farrant 2014), upon completion, students should be competent in conducting basic qualitative research.

They are required to have the knowledge of research principles and the skills for independent research, yet, students often struggle with this and see research as a frightening and mysterious activity conducted only by academics (McCarthy 2015). The awareness of the explicit research end product is not difficult. There is a clear, physical outcome- the dissertation.

The difficulty lies in the hidden and secret (Farrant 2014) research process. How to start? What to do? How to plan? The complexity can be difficult for students to understand, for supervisors to articulate and has been called a 'concealed journey' (Ferrance 2000).

The conceptualisation of research as a journey is longstanding. Students begin their journey with a naïve interest in a topic and over time, construct knowledge about the research process itself (Mackenzie and Ling 2009). This tacit, or practical research knowledge lies below the surface and is traditionally accumulated only through experience and learning by doing (Mlambo 2014). As an academic and research supervisor, the author recognised the experiences the students had of the research journey itself were invaluable (Farrant 2014). However, once students completed their dissertation and graduated, this knowledge was lost and not accessible to others. The challenge, therefore, was how to capture and 'teach' this tacit knowledge or practical intelligence, acquired through the research experience itself. I realised one way of doing this was for past students to share stories which can help make individual, implicit knowledge public (Mascitelli 2000). However, I was unsure of the best platform to capture these stories or how to preserve them as resources to help make meaning of the research journey. This led directly to the aim and specific objectives of this innovation:

Aim
To create sustainable resources that help academics unveil the hidden research 'process' to students.

Objectives:
- To critically evaluate current storytelling technologies and software
- To collate past student work and create research stories
- To include all stakeholder views in each stage of development
- To minimize time and cost to academics in the creation of these stories
- To evaluate the initiative from all stakeholders positions

2. Problem to Solve
Along the research journey, our students, like others on similar programmes, submit small pieces of work as milestones of progress and academics provide feedback on this work. This includes two draft proposals, PowerPoint presentations, chapter submissions and oral presentations. Although, this is all held electronically (including the oral presentations as they are recorded), current students only have access to select parts of this past work and there is no organisation, narrative or cohesion. For example, students can come in and look at past research proposals or physical copies of submitted dissertations. They can search a central database for the recordings. These, however are only atomistic parts of past research products, in isolation. Both the overall student experiences, changes in direction, struggles and solutions combined with past academic guidance given, are not easily accessible and therefore, lost.

As these valuable resources are archived electronically, I recognized if these could be organised, collated and presented to students, it could help demonstrate the evolution and complexity of the research process.

However, as an academic, I was also fully aware that lack of time is the leading barrier to development of resources for academics (Walker 2016). I began to investigate digital storytelling, which links the age-old concept of storytelling to technology by combining the idea of telling stories with a variety of multimedia tools. Digital stories are not new and have been used widely to share material, subjects, topics and content. They have tremendous potential (Robin 2008), but have been almost totally overlooked as a platform for fostering and transferring embedded and tacit knowledge (Ambrosini and Bowman 2001, Mlambo 2014).

2.1 Teaching Innovation

Therefore, in an effort to make the tacit research process explicit, I created research digistories (RDS) as online educational resources for current students. They are organised, step-by-step examples, using past student milestones submitted with academic feedback already given along with a central narrative. These multimedia stories were created using existing, archived materials. The academic created the example below; the template, now developed, is being populated by an administrator.

3. Methods and Infrastructure

One of the first challenges was choosing the right software. After researching what was available, a survey was conducted to further refine the choice. Participants included technicians, students, teachers and administrators. The results suggested the software had to be accessible, compatible, not bespoke, easy to use and the artefacts produced had to be 'shareable'. Therefore, the digital storytelling software 'Sway' was chosen, which enables users to create and share interactive reports or presentations and is fully editable. As a commercial product, it is user friendly, basic and similar to PowerPoint in use. It is accessible on desktop and mobile devices. Most importantly, it is fully integrated with all Office 365 applications, the most common productivity software in the UK and is a market leader for productivity apps in Europe and North America.

The academic contacted a past student and after receiving permission, collated all of their work and academic feedback from the University's archives and created the first draft RDS. In total, three focus groups including all stakeholders, (technicians, students and research supervisors) were held to decide a final template. After the first focus group (n=12), we were faced with a challenge as what we initially thought students would find valuable was very different from what they told us. Originally, in the first template, the stories were unconstrained and students could explore

Laura Delgaty

and move through them however they chose. Yet, feedback from students unanimously suggested they wanted a linear story, with no options for deviation. Furthermore, they wanted an index with links to each research section at the beginning and the end of the RDS. This feedback was invaluable and we created a second draft based on this. Using this draft template, five further student research journeys were purposively chosen to be transformed into RDS. Literature suggests that showing students examples of past work that is only of a meritorious standard can actually be destructive to self- confidence and motivation (Biggs 2011). It is important for students to see cross sections of work, including fails.

Therefore, a further challenge was gaining permission from a student who failed in the past to share their work, grades and feedback openly.

However, it was explained to the student that we did not only want meritorious examples. We were trying to demonstrate the complexity, and perhaps difficulty of independent research. The student generously agreed. Therefore these five RDS included a cross section of projects, including particularly strong and weak dissertations. The academic feedback and mark are included at each stage, so for current students, they will have access to a range of past student work. The written, academic feedback and actual grade in situ may help facilitate explanation and to make the process explicit.

Therefore, archived work and past academic feedback was collated, organised and five RDS were created using the updated template. These were exported to the individual students, who were asked to review their entire research journeys and create a short reflective narrative. These reflective narratives were added to the final RDS to create a coherent account of each student's experience of the research process. These were shared with a second focus group (n=8) for feedback. The final RDS are not anonymous. This was another challenge to the development as we originally ensured there was nothing identifiable in the stories and went to extreme lengths in editing to ensure this anonymity. However, in the second focus group, past students, proud of their accomplishments asked that their names and photos be included. The template was modified again in response to this unanimous feedback. Interestingly, this corresponds to literature, suggesting sharing RDS is a way to publicise work and fosters social learning amongst peers (Mlambo 2014). One copy of the final five

RDS was sent to past students for their own dissemination, corresponding to the author's personal and institutional aim of facilitating students to share and present their research. Another copy, including the final narrative, was uploaded as a resource in our password protected learning environment for current students and supervisors. There were no explicit task or instructions. Students and supervisors were directed there to view them, however, whenever and how ever often they chose. This iterative process from initial to final draft took approximately 6 months.

4. How the initiative was received

Identifying and measuring student impact is essential. Interestingly, although RDS have been widely used, there is almost a total lack of evaluation (Robin 2008, Biggs 2011). Impact has been monitored by collecting both quantitative and qualitative data from different stakeholders: current and past students, supervisors and the institution.

4.1. Quantitative data evaluation

Quantitative data, using web analytics, when used in combination with other outcomes, can become meaningful and actionable (Rogers, McEwan et al. 2010) whilst offering a depiction of student behaviour online. With an average of 300 direct hits per month (cohort of 20 students), and over 3500 in the first academic year, clearly these are being used often, and regularly. Although it would be dangerous to interpret such small numbers statistically, last academic year (the first these were available to students as resources) we had one student who was given an unsatisfactory mark in his work. In past years, we have had up to 9 students who received unsatisfactory as clearly their work did not demonstrate achievement of the module learning outcomes. Tentative and early inferences may suggest that the availability of these resources may have significantly impacted overall pass rates and therefore increased successful demonstration of the learning outcomes for these students.

4.2. Qualitative data evaluation

Qualitative free text data from 2 separate formal evaluations and a third focus group (n=8) to evaluate the end product was overwhelmingly positive and feedback from students includes: 'Seeing the process itself was so incredibly valuable, I go back to them again and again', 'I looked at these at least once a week as I progressed with my research ideas at each step. It was like a map.... better than a map. It really helped my see the bigger picture and check my progress' and 'Spent hours looking at these…made me realise how complex/non-linear the research process is. Honestly, they were a fantastic resource'.

At our annual research supervisor meeting, the RDS were viewed and discussed and supervisor feedback incudes 'What a great use of academic time and student work. A wonderful, explicit resource that has been staring us in the face!'

The author was asked to present this innovation as a training workshop institutionally. There was significant interest, so the template developed for this programme was shared openly. Three other non-related programmes have slightly altered the template and are using it to create RDS for their students. It has also been shared with other two other Masters programmes nationally and implemented for their programmes. The enthusiastic uptake by other programmes suggests this is a shareable template and an effective and valuable resource.

5. Plans to further develop the initiative
This is a work in progress. The RDS continue to be created and shared with students. The value to students is continuing to be evaluated. How and when supervisors use them, and when they direct students to them is also being monitored.

More detailed analytics are being collected related to assessment results. These will be analysed longitudinally to demonstrate a significant correlation. The author is in discussion with two other related Maters programmes at different institutions nationally who are implementing RDS for their students. Our plan goal is to not just share the RDS with cohorts at our local institutions, but to try and develop a central repository to share students RDS cross-intuitionally as learning resources.

Unequivocally, measuring knowledge, skills and development in students whilst in Higher Education is essential, yet increasingly difficult. As a result, the HEA (Higher Education Academy) are currently encouraging research that measures the improvement of these elements, labelled Learning Gain.

After disseminating the RDS innovation locally, the author has been invited to join a national inter-institutional team and apply for an HEA funding

Laura Delgaty

award. The aim is to utilise RDS and ideas from this innovation, specifically the student's reflective components, to demonstrate and perhaps measure Learning Gain.

6. Conclusion

This teaching innovation responds to student need, a gap in current published practice and academic pressures. It is fully editable, exportable, and the RDS can be created by administrators, saving valuable academic time. Most importantly there is clear evidence, this easily transferable and sustainable innovation is helping academics unveil, and students make sense of, the hidden and implicit research process.

Please click here (allowing a minute to load) to view a RDS example: https://sway.com/Knh6K3mIsIMsnnjs

References

Ambrosini, V. and C. Bowman (2001). "Tacit knowledge: Some suggestions for operationalization." Journal of Management Studies 38(6): 811-829.

Biggs, J. B. (2011). Teaching for quality learning at university: What the student does, McGraw-Hill Education (UK).

Farrant, F. (2014). "Unconcealment What Happens When We Tell Stories." Qualitative Inquiry 20(4): 461-470.

Ferrance, E. (2000). Action Research- Themes in Education. Northease and Islands Regional Educational Laboratory. B. University. Providence, RI, Brown University: 1-33.

Lewis, P. J. (2011). "Storytelling as research/research as storytelling." Qualitative Inquiry 17(6): 505-510.

Mackenzie, N. and L. Ling (2009). "The research journey: A Lonely Planet approach." Issues in Educational Research 19(1): 48-60.

Mascitelli, R. (2000). "From experience: harnessing tacit knowledge to achieve breakthrough innovation." Journal of product innovation management 17(3): 179-193.

McCarthy, G. (2015). "Motivating and enabling adult learners to develop research skills." Australian Journal of Adult Learning 55(2): 309.

Mlambo, S. (2014). "Using digital storytelling to externalise personal knowledge of research processes: The case of a Knowledge Audio repository." The Internet and Higher Education 22: 11-23.

Robin, B. R. (2008). The effective uses of digital storytelling as a teaching and learning tool. Handbook of research on teaching literacy through the communicative and visual arts (Vol. 2). New York, Lawrence Erlbaum Associates.

Rogers, P., et al. (2010). The Use of Web Analytics in the Design and Evaluation of Distance Education. Using emerging technologies in distance education G. Veletsianos. Athabaska, Athabaska University Press: 231-247.

Walker, R., Voce, J, Swift, E, Ahmed, J, Jenkins,M, Vincent,P (2016). 2016 Survey of Technology Enhanced Learning for highereducation in the UK. UCISA. Oxford, Universtiy of Oxford: 1-222.

Author Biography

Laura Delgaty is a physiotherapist, with a Master's and Doctoral Degree in education. Her thesis investigated the implementation of distance learning programmes for clinicians. Currently, as Deputy Degree Programme Director and Senior Lecturer on Newcastle University's Medical Education Programme, her areas of research include: technology, medical education, diversity and curricular studies.

Live-Teaching and Live-Learning with alfaview®: Creating an economical, ecological and social shift with live e-Learning

Niko Fostiropoulos, Vaia Rapti and Armin Schweinfurth
alfatraining Bildungszentrum GmbH, Germany
niko.fostiropoulos@alfatraining.de
vaia.rapti@alfatraining.de
armin.schweinfurth@alfatraining.de

1. Introduction

alfatraining Bildungszentrum is a labour market-oriented company offering advanced vocational training. Since its foundation in 2005, the educational company has grown to 66 locations in Germany, one location in Greece, 330 employees and 180 freelance lecturers. alfatraining qualifies in all fields relevant to the labour market. The advanced training courses are IT-related and government-funded.

In 2010, the company was faced with the challenge that the costs for lecturers and classrooms were an obstacle to growth. At the same time, lecturers and participants had to travel long distances to the training centers and the inclusion of physically handicapped people, such as the hearing-impaired, in the lessons was difficult. This situation led to the following triangle of goals:

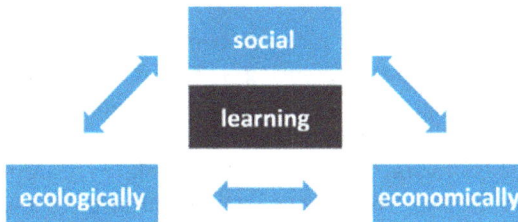

Figure 1: Three goals with live e-Learning

The introduction of video technology was intended to solve all the challenges to achieve the following:

social	economically	ecologically
• Reduce the start guarantee of the courses to four weeks to enable a quick career jump • Improve learning quality through new live e-Learning methods • Barrier-free learning & inclusion (e.g. support the deaf with sign language) • Enabling learning for people with children and single parents	• New locations in rural areas to reach all people • Simplification of communication within the EU locations (Germany & Greece) • Reduce costs per location • Easier EU-wide recruiting of lecturers • Internationalisation of education	• No more journeys for lecturers • time saving through learning at home • Enable learning from home

In order to achieve the above-mentioned goals, alfatraining focused on digitizing the training using live video technology. In the training department, classes are now held for participants via lip-synchronous live video transmission. As the existing videoconferencing solutions on the market were not satisfactory, alfatraining developed its own videoconferencing system: alfaview®. An in-house team of software developers in Germany and Greece has programmed the video conferencing system and is continuously driving its further development. To date, more than 40,000 people have received training in 200 advanced training courses. Currently, more than 2000 people are taught with alfaview every day.

2. Infrastructure

Software
The heart of the digital initiative is the alfaview videoconferencing software. In comparison to other videoconferencing solutions, alfaview grants real-time collaboration with the highest quality in audio and video while all participants in a videoconference can communicate and work together in real time. To date, there is no comparable software that makes it possible to transmit 100 or more participant videos live, lip-synchronous, stable and in the same high video and audio quality.

Niko Fostiropoulos, Vaia Rapti and Armin Schweinfurth

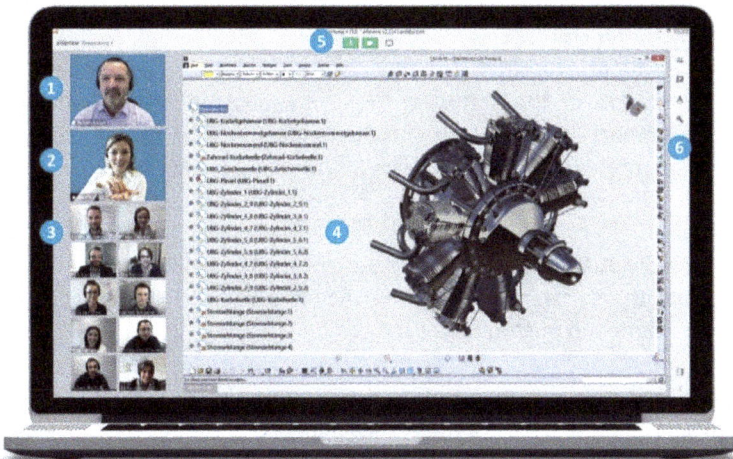

Figure 2: alfaview surface

1. Lecturer
The videostream oft the instructor takes place in an enlarged video window. This ensures that all participants take up the aspects of the teacher's non-verbal communication (facial expressions and gestures), which improves the learning experience and sustainably increases the quality of learning.

2. Sign Translator
In order to ensure accessibility and, for example, the inclusion of the hearing-impaired, it is possible that a sign language interpreter can be transferred within alfaview. Due to the high-resolution video quality, even with a high number of videos, the sign language communication is always clearly visible.

3. Participants
Under the sign language interpreters' video, the participants are also transmitted live and lip-synchronously in the highest video quality. The participant videos as well as the instructor video are marked with names, which makes it easier to address each other.

4. Screen sharing
An intuitive user interface allows participants to share their own screens with all other participants so that they can view presentations and i.e. software demonstrations. The special thing about it is that not only the instructor's screen but also that of the participants can be shared tot he same time. This makes it easier to check and correct the tasks of the participants.

79

5.   Intuitive controls

During the development of alfaview, special emphasis is placed on the simple and intuitive operation of the software. The conscious reduction to the essential operating elements and the clean and tidy appearance helps the participants to familiarize themselves with the software in the shortest time.

6.   Settings

In order to individualize the learning experience with alfaview, each participant is free to adapt the software to his or her needs. For example, the color scheme, language, camera and microphone used can be changed.

Room concept

Following the intuitive user interface, the room concept will be explained in more detail below. alfaview relies on a room concept instead of a moderator concept. In classic video conferencing solutions, a moderator has to set up a room, start it and invite the participants before a video conference can be started. alfaview offers the participants fixed rooms that can be entered directly by lecturers and participants. Time-consuming allocation of rights and invitation practices become superfluous. The room interface is explained in more detail below:

Figure 3: alfaview room view

1.   Enter room

Participants enter the appropriate room via the user interface. Of course, it is possible to control which persons have access to individual training rooms via the allocation of rights.

2.   Room name and training topic

To give the participants a quick overview of their respective training rooms, the training area and room name are clearly displayed on the user interface.

3. Favourites

Each participant has the possibility to favour the suitable rooms with one click. These are displayed first in the room selection.

4. Number of participants

To see who is in a room, you can see the number of participants and with mouseover the names of learners.

People

A wide variety of stakeholders are involved in alfatraining and alfaview's live e-Learning concept.

Management Team

The management, in the person of Niko Fostiropoulos, is the driving innovator behind digital initiative and the further development of alfaview. Together with the members of the leadership team and in coordination with the developers, the management prioritizes the alignment of the software and its functions in order to constantly optimize the live e-learning experience for the participants. The management attaches great importance to the fact that ecological, economic and social goals are achieved through the use of the software.

Developers

The development of alfaview is carried out by an EU-wide development team in Stuttgart (Germany) and Thessaloniki (Greece). The international team consists of 15 developers. In addition to the further development of the software, the team also provides advice on alfaview at events, trade fairs and presentations.

Training Organisation

To ensure that the training courses run smoothly, there are several training organisers throughout Germany who can log on directly to the relevant training rooms in alfaview if questions arise. Instead of having a physical presence per location, several locations can be managed by smaller teams (alfateams), resulting in increased efficiency for the training organization. Furthermore, the training organisers exchange information centrally in alfaview, which facilitates communication and maintains team spirit even over long distances.

Participants

All participants in advanced education throughout Germany are connected with the interactive live learning platform. The lessons take place with a live video stream which enables audiovisual communication and interaction: They see and hear each other, can give immediate feedback and are able to ask the lecturer questions at any time.

The teaching is comparable to traditional face-to-face teaching, only with the difference that nobody is physically present in a room. All participating persons of a advanced education course work with two screens. On the first monitor, the image, sound and screen of the lecturer and the other participants are transmitted in high quality. On the second screen, the participant works on his or her own training project. The participants are located at one of alfatraining's training centres at 65 locations in Germany or learn and work from home. For the entire duration of the course, alfatraining provides the home participants with a laptop and a second monitor.

Lectures

Like the participants, the lecturers also conduct the lessons locally. alfatraining offers the possibility for the lecturers from local broadcasting centres to log on to alfaview and conduct the lessons. However, lecturers are increasingly taking the opportunity to teach from home via alfaview in the home office. This development not only saves space and infrastructure costs for the company, but also helps the lecturers to save travel time and travel costs.

3. Technical Challenges

During the development of alfaview there were two main challenges that were critical for the success of the project. On the one hand, the task of the developers was that alfaview enables lip-synchronous transmission of audio and video signals even at low bandwidths. On the other hand, another challenge was to create a solution that, in contrast to known products, enables a 24/7 - non-stop use of the video conferencing software with the highest stability, so that video conferences can also be held with 100+ participants around the clock.

Figure 4: Quality of videostream

The approach of being able to offer audio and video transmission even at low bandwidths is based on the desire that education should be made accessible anywhere in the world. Education must not be an urban monopoly. Especially in rural areas, perhaps not equipped with high bandwidth, alfaview is to be used as well as in larger cities.

The stability of audio and video transmission serves above all to ensure learning quality. alfaview is the only system that offers the possibility of enriching learning with non-verbal aspects such as gestures and facial expressions. This requires stable transmission of video and audio signals. This ensures that the deaf, for example, can also be taught with the integration of a video stream for sign language.

In order to meet these challenges, alfaview's infrastructure was fundamentally redeveloped and specially adapted. Today, participants have the option of adapting alfaview to their individual bandwidth. The required stability was also achieved during the five-year development period, so that today more than 2000 participants are taught every day in the highest audio and video quality with alfaview Live e-Learning.

4. How the initiative was received

As with any digital initiative, there is a certain scepticism at the beginning among the people involved. This is also the case with alfaview. At the beginning, the lecturers were certain that their classical face-to-face teaching with beamer, blackboard and overhead projector could not be digitized and that digital teaching would have disadvantages. The participants were also sceptical, as they had never known such a learning format before. The question that arose was:

"Do the lecturers and participants accept this new form of teaching?"

In order to anticipate any negative developments, a test period of four weeks was agreed with the lecturers, during which they were to test and evaluate the new type of teaching and then contribute their experiences to a constructive feedback process. After four weeks all lecturers agreed that this form of decentralized teaching only has advantages for you and the participants. The high audio and video quality ensures that the lessons are the same as face-to-face lessons, without having to accept the disadvantages (journey, travel costs, etc.) of a classical form of teaching. In addition, other flexible lecturers can be deployed via alfaview in the event of illness.

The participants also quickly got used to the new teaching method and actively ask whether the digital form of teaching is described in their certificates. They know that their future employers are looking for digitally experienced employees and prefer to learn with alfaview. Thanks to the intuitive usage of the software, even PC beginners can work with alfaview in less than 30 minutes.

By using the alfaview® live video platform, more people have access to training, regardless of their location, physical condition or social circumstances.

Furthermore, alfaview is also successful in internal corporate communication. All employees of alfatraining communicate with each other with alfaview. The results are very positive: The meeting times were significantly shortened and the quality of the internal communication was sustainably increased. New employees also use alfaview right from the start to communicate with their colleagues.

5. The learning outcomes

We are convinced that education contributes to social justice. The aim of the initiative was and still is to overcome ecological, economic and social hurdles in order to make education possible in all regions of the EU. According to this case study, alfatraining is working with alfaview on the following mission:

"We see education as a great asset of our society and as the basis for social justice. It is our concern to develop high-quality IT training courses and to sustainably support people in their professional training. Our goal is to promote IT knowledge to actively participate in shaping labour market-related standards. By the barrier-free qualification of humans over video technology the quality in the knowledge transfer is lastingly increased".

What changes have taken place since the digital initiative?

The use of the alfaview video platform in the training area has made internal company processes more ecological and user-friendly. Success is measured by different KPIs and is reflected in the reduced Time To Market (TTM) and increased Customer Lifetime Value (CLV) of the course participants.

Furthermore, all departments enjoy the advantages of the additional communication tool alfaview®, which maintains team spirit even across locations further apart. A clear development in the use of alfaview shows the development of the locations with the aim of transporting education to all regions.

Niko Fostiropoulos, Vaia Rapti and Armin Schweinfurth

Since the introduction of video technology in 2010, alfatraining has grown from 10 to 66 locations and is helping more and more people in their professional development:

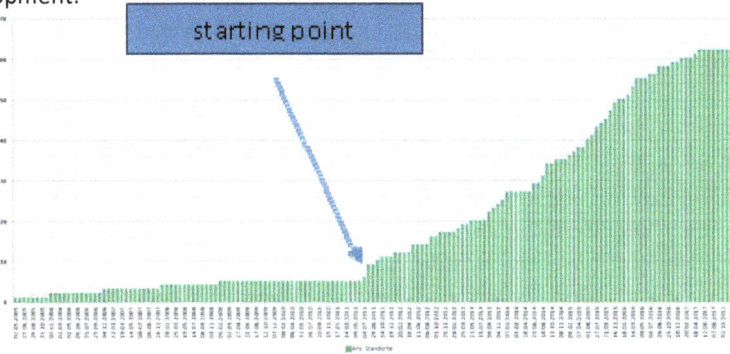

Figure 5: Growth rate of alfatraining branches from 2000 to 2017

The ecological, economic and social barriers for our participants and lecturers have been sustainably reduced. Participants with physical disabilities now have the opportunity to actively participate in the training courses. Teachers save long journeys, stress and valuable time as they can teach from home. Satisfaction among training participants and lecturers has risen sustainably and alfaview has established itself as a live e-learning platform for further training.

We have also learned that live e-learning can be used on several levels: At alfatraning we use live e-learning with alfaview for training our participants and internal staff training. Other companies can also use the software to simplify the training of their employees. On a third level, alfaview is also used by universities and distance learning colleges to provide their students with stable, high-quality teaching.

Figure 6: Three levels of usage

85

6. Summary and plans to further develop the initiative

With the use of alfaview live e-Learning in training and for the entire internal communication, the company alfatraining has been able to continuously expand its training offers in recent years and to network the growing number of locations in Germany and Greece in a stable manner.

The optimized communication situation in the company improves existing workflows and leads to an efficient implementation of all projects. The multimedia networking via video technology removes the regional limitation of course participation and gives the company the opportunity to plan seminars more efficiently. The own course portfolio can be offered independent of location. Furthermore, people in rural regions also benefit from alfatraining's continuing education programmes.

Video technology makes it possible to recruit the most qualified lecturers for the seminars from any location.

alfaview® also offers further options - for example in the area of barrier-free integration and qualification. With alfaview® it is possible for deaf people to add a sign language interpreter live to the course. This enables the inclusion of deaf and hearing-impaired participants and colleagues.

In 2018, international research projects and collaborations were initiated together with the Karlsruhe Institute of Technology (KIT) and a multilingual live translator will be integrated into alfaview® to translate and transcribe sessions. alfatraining.com a webshop for worldwide private advanced is now live and oofers private advanced eduction in english language to people in and outside of Germany. A national job exchange for graduates of the sponsored advanced education is already in the concept phase for the year 2019.

The further digitization of e-learning processes and the digitization of the company are very strongly integrated into the corporate strategy. The new digital strategy of the management provides for active participation in shaping the digital transformation and leading to the dematerialisation of learning materials and administration. The use of alfaview® in training and corporate communications has resulted in significant savings in travel costs, working hours and training costs for several years, while at the same time optimising the ecological, economic and social factors for the company, the training participants and all 330 employees.

Contributing Author Biographies:

Vaia Rapti is head coordinator for international projects and brings her extensive multinational experience to the company alfatraining, especially in the field of public relations. She represents the company at trade fairs at in Germany and abroad and is responsible for the coordination of all international projects.

Niko Fostiropoulos founded the educational company alfatraining® in 2004 and developed it into one of the most successful educational companies in Germany, especially through the use of the video technology alfaview® (www.alfaview.com). Since 2018, it has provided the online seminar platform www.alfatraining.com, which can be used to attend live video courses worldwide.

Armin Schweinfurth is Head of Business Development and brings in his national and international expertise in Digitization, Sales and Business Development. He is responsible for the presentation of alfaview and continues to lead two EU projects in which alfatraining works together with different universities in digitisation projects.

Crossteaching Interuniversity Research-Based Learning in Virtual Teams

Michael A. Herzog[1], Elisabeth Katzlinger-Felhofer[2,] Martin Stabauer[2] and
Leonore Franz[1]
[1]Magdeburg-Stendal University, Germany
[2]Johannes Kepler University Linz, Austria
Michael.herzog@hs-magdeburg.de
Leonore.franz@hs-magdeburg.de
elisabeth.katzlinger@jku.at
martin.stabauer@jku.at

Abstract: Since 2010 we are developing learning settings which s(t)imulate virtual collaboration in the globalized professional world. Students from two universities in different countries cooperate in virtual learning teams. The most recent setting is an inquiry-based learning scenario concerned with scientific paper writing. Master's students from different majors and universities work together in virtual teams, define their own research objects and process a full research cycle from drafting a proposal over executing research to writing a paper and presenting it at an academic conference. The technical infrastructure design for collaboration is set with the learning management system Moodle for peer review and team building, video conferencing for feedback from the teachers, as well as other tools like shared spaces or telecommunication for group communication. We faced challenges, especially regarding students' behaviour as well as their intercultural and professional diversity, but also organizational barriers in interuniversity collaboration. To cope with these challenges, variations of learning opportunities and additional online support were offered. As the scenario is driven by four teachers in three Master programs at three universities, the intention was to create a special interdisciplinary online experience that is particularly suitable for students with a job. Student evaluations show, that electronic tools and our learning methods helped to fit the online scenario better to this group than through classic classroom learning. The evaluation consisted of an online survey (n>900) and group reflection papers written by students. While the scenario addresses almost all of taxonomies of learning, the digital skillset that the students learn ranges from media to information literacy, communication and collaboration skills to e-Learning and reflection skills. The initiative and the learning scenario are further driven by the introduction of a new joint online study program, for part time working students in Digital Business Management, and the establishment of a lab, where we can develop eye tracking and face reader studies to investigate the use of tools in our setting.

89

1. Introduction

The presented learning scenario is based on an intensive collaboration of higher education institutions in two countries. In the winter term of 2010 the »CrossTeaching« learning scenario was established, in which students of the involved institutions worked together in virtual learning groups. The learning setting simulates the virtual collaboration in the globalized professional world. Starting in the winter term 2015 the advanced inquiry-based learning setting on scientific paper writing was developed, which is described in this work. Students of three different majors cooperate and work out a paper on the generic topic »Interdisciplinary Reflection of Ethical Issues in Digital Communication«. The focus of this inquiry-based learning scenario is to improve students' collaboration skills, media literacy and competency for interdisciplinary work in virtual teams by working together on a research project.

This initiative deals with an interuniversity collaboration between the Johannes Kepler University (JKU) Linz, Austria, and the Magdeburg-Stendal University of Applied Sciences, Germany. The involved master's programs are Digital Business Management (a cooperation of the University of Applied Sciences Upper Austria (FHOÖ), Campus Steyr, and JKU Linz), Risk Management and Cross Media (both Stendal and Magdeburg). Interinstitutional and interdisciplinary cooperation is a hallmark of all participating programs. Digital Business Management is Austria's first ever Master programme that is jointly conducted by an University of Applied Sciences and a research-based University. The curriculum is structured by one half of its courses run at JKU in Linz and one half at the FHOÖ in Steyr. Students are enrolled in both institutions and use the respective learning platforms.

This cooperation is the basic condition for the collaboration of students in virtual learning groups. Four teachers and courses are involved in the learning setting. Students built interuniversity learning groups out of two or three students from Linz and one or two students from Magdeburg or Stendal depending on the number of students in the courses. In total around 45 students participate each year. Most of the involved students are part-time students and work up to 40 hours/week. The distance between the institutions is 750 km. Therefore, it is obvious that students cooperate mostly online.

The first step in the process (figure 1) is an online kickoff for introducing the learning setting. Then the four teachers and the students meet in "breakout rooms" in small groups to discuss potential research topics. In the next phase, students find their learning groups via the forum of Moodle.

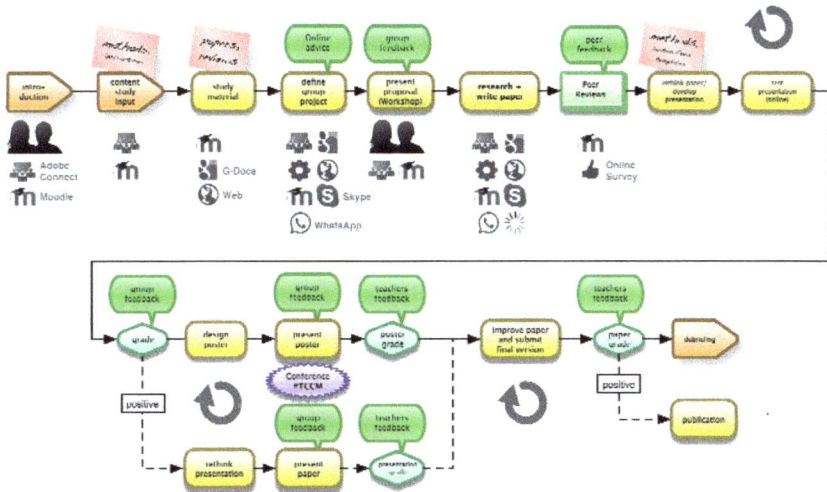

Figure 1: Advanced inquiry-based learning process model (Herzog, Katzlinger, Stabauer, 2016)

In the learning group, students start their research process by discussing and finding their research question corresponding to the generic topic. Parallel to this discussion process in the different courses, students get input regarding research methods or ethical issues via face-to-face meetings or online sessions. At the end of this discussion process, research proposals are presented at a one-day face-to-face research workshop, which takes place in Linz. At this workshop, most group members meet personally for the first time. While they have time to organize their research process, they also get a lot of feedback from teachers and other students about their proposal.

In the next phase, students conduct their research. This is accompanied by online group sessions with the teachers. Learning groups get more feedback about questions, progress and methodology. These online sessions are voluntary for the students, but they are well accepted and important for the subsequent research process. At the end of this phase, research and findings are documented in a full conference paper that has to be submitted for peer review. As usual at scientific conferences, all student reviewers give peer feedback and evaluate other papers. The review process is the basis for the decision which paper is presented as a talk or a poster at the scientific conference "Think Cross – Change Media (#TCCM)" in Magdeburg. This conference is the second formal chance for face-to-face meetings of all learning groups and also a major incentive for students: The chances of presenting at a "real" scientific conference and having a paper published in the conference proceedings turned out to be very motivating. Comments of the peer reviews and also from the conference are incorporated into the final version of the paper. The best papers are published in the conference proceedings after the conference.

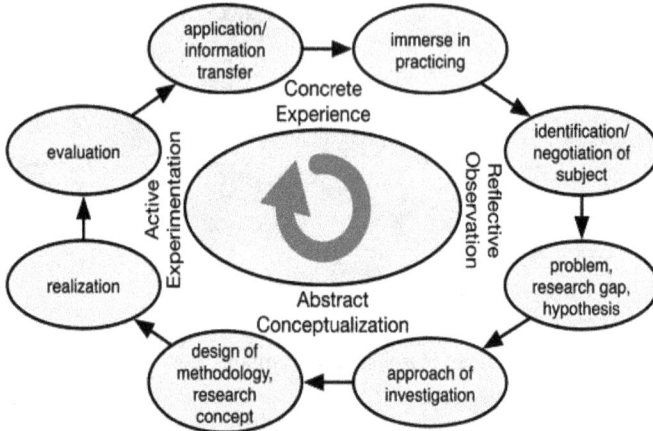

Figure 2: Kolb´s Learning Cycle synchronised with Wildt´s Research Cycle (Wildt, 2009)

The whole process of the initiative is designed according to Wildt´s research cycle aligned with Kolb´s experience-based learning model (Wildt, 2009; Kolb, 1995).

Wildt developed a model which allows to synchronize the research process according to the learning development (figure 2). This way the inquiry-based learning method addresses specifically the cognitive processes of the students. In our setting the learning process begins with a concrete experience though an observation of work practice or the assessment of the current state of research in a particular field. Therefore, the student groups discuss their ideas and find an appropriate topic. Then the groups develop relevant research questions and/or hypotheses and discuss the primary findings (reflective observation). During the phase of abstract conceptualization the students create adequate research designs and choose suitable research methods. Afterwards the students collect information or respectively create a prototype (active experimentation) they analyse the data or evaluate their sample (Herzog, Katzlinger, Stabauer, 2016).

2. The infrastructure

Our project combines a wide variety of learning and collaboration tools (figure 3) to establish unique personal learning experiences. Students start from a common Moodle course (mandatory, every student accesses from different universities) and they themselves choose the collaboration tools for their group work. Adobe Connect as a Web-conference platform is used and demonstrated for class interconnection over the whole course. This platform is hosted by DFN, a German federal institution with excellent internet connection. We provide recordings from online-sessions for asynchronous access. Students can use the tool as moderators whenever they need it.

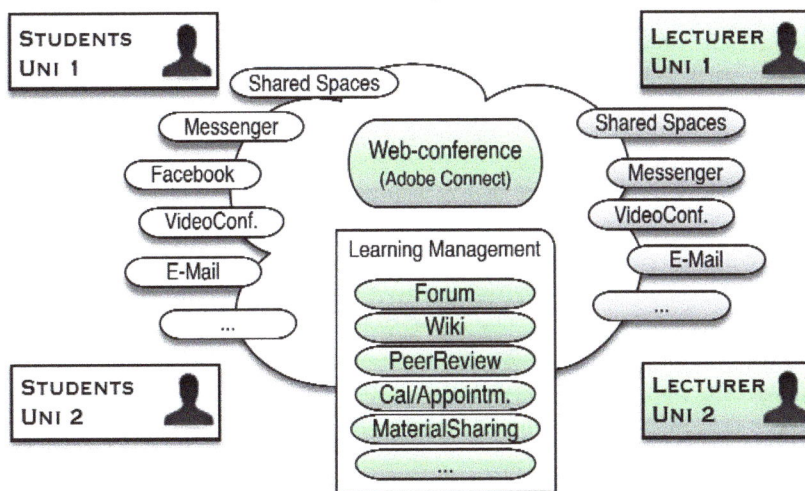

Figure 3: Tools in use for virtual collaboration

We investigated the usage and usefulness of collaborative media according to student ratings (figure 4). The learning groups were responsible for their own organization of group work, choice of tools and communication media and choosing or creating their appropriate methodology for their respective research question. This resulted in a broad variety of research methods and approaches. Nevertheless, teachers support regarding research methods, a research workshop with discussions of all research proposals, as well as online consulting was highly used and valued.

Face-to-face is still the preferred communication channel, whereas chat and forum became less important, and social media and video conference gained more importance. Since 2015, students preferred shared spaces like Google Docs, Microsoft OneDrive, or Dropbox with a very high rating (3.9 of 4). With these results we are able to reconsider and adopt the blend of e-Learning tools in every new course.

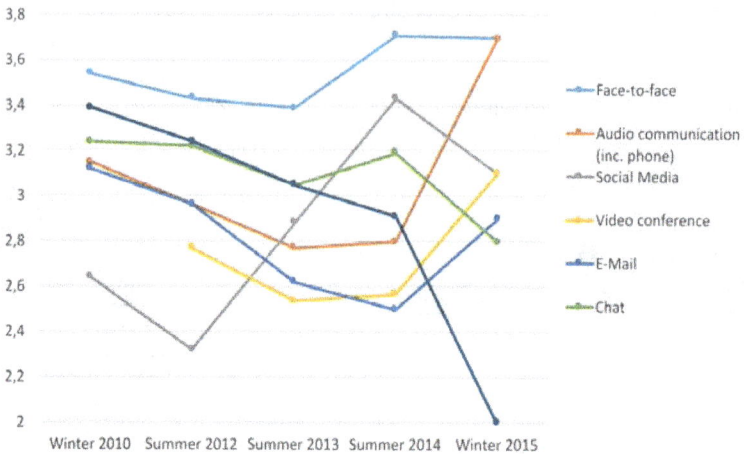

Figure 4: Rating of media for collaboration [1] not useful, [4] very useful; n<900 (Herzog, Katzlinger, Stabauer 2016)

3. The challenges

Although the described learning scenario was perceived very well by all parties involved (see next chapter), some challenges did emerge during the lifecycle of the project. First of all, the scenario was set up with a reduction of the lecturers' workload in mind as one of the aims. Due to the variety of online and offline contact points and the high level of support, this intention was not yet reached. The consistently satisfying results make up for this point, though.

Financing of the different dates and options of physical presence was another challenge. While most of the lecturers' traveling costs were covered by the ERASMUS+ program, the students did not have that option and had to bring in their own resources. We kept these dates optional as some of the students were not able to attend. Additionally, all study programs are designed for working professionals, which has implications on periods of face-to-face training and on the availability for group meetings.

The students' interdisciplinarity brought a great variety to the applied research methods, tools and approaches, and it enabled the diversity of research projects within the learning scenario. However, it also brought additional complexity and some difficulties in communication. Interestingly enough, a few groups also experienced some form of language barrier between their members' dialects (i.e. Austrian German and German German). Cultural differences made the groupwork both interesting and challenging for many groups. Habitual structures were broken through and the students had to adopt new mindsets and attitudes.

Another issue was the courses' differences in credits given and positioning in the curricula. While the students of Digital Business Management received 3 ECTS per course, adding up to 6 ECTS in total, the students from Magdeburg only received 5 ECTS for their modules. For reasons that are easy to sympathize with, this led to discussions among the students. However, the difference can be justified simply as the courses in Linz required additional classwork outside the described learning scenario.

Figure 5: KickOff Meeting in the Web-conference system Adobe Connect

Lastly, occasional technical issues occurred. Adobe Connect was used throughout the course, and during the kickoff meeting the number of connections exceeded 40 (figure 5). This principally worked quite well, but it also sets the bar very high for all participants when it comes to discipline regarding microphone usage and clicking on various buttons. A small number of students also complained about technical problems during the group work and the feedback meetings.

4. Feedback from the participants

"Although the preparation of this paper was as exhausting as no other task during my studies, I would recommend this cooperation with the Magdeburg-Stendal University for the next years. We have gained another experience, it's also interesting to see that students from another university sometimes have quite different approaches."

The evaluation of the learning scenario is based on an online survey (n>900) and group reflection papers written by the students. In our online survey, the students rated the usefulness of different media they used in the learning scenario as shown in figure 3. Online peer review as a learning method was rated on average with 3.4 on a four-point Likert scale (4...excellent).

"Working with virtual teams is an enrichment for all of us, even if it's not always easy - an experience that can also be helpful in today's working life."

For the evaluation process every student had to write a learning diary and a reflection paper about the cooperation in the learning group. The quotes presented in this chapter provide an insight into the general atmosphere among the students. The diaries also show that the virtual teambuilding process was a challenge for the students. However, after the first storming phase, the interdisciplinary cooperation leads to a positive learning outcome.

"Scientific paper writing is a very exciting learning method. Especially the interdisciplinary cooperation is something that you usually do not do during your studies. It is highly recommended also in terms of conflict prevention and conflict resolution."

5. The learning outcomes
At least five cognitive domains of Bloom's Taxonomy (Bloom et al, 1956; Anderson et al, 2001) are addressed in the learning scenario – comprehending, applying, analysing, evaluating and creating. At the beginning of the learning process the students need to understand, explain and discuss their ideas for the paper, to then formulate a potential research topic (comprehending). Afterwards they sketch a draft of their paper, conduct research and formulate their research method (applying). However, the learning scenario aims to especially address the higher domains of Bloom's Taxonomy. By writing their paper they draw connections among different ideas and test these (analysing), interpret their results and draw conclusions (evaluating). The continuous peer reviews involve the critical examination of the other students draft presentations or papers' according to pre-set criteria. Thereby they also differentiate which of the presentations or papers comply to a scientific character (analysing). On this basis they formulate their constructive critique and make well-founded statements about the quality of the presentation or paper (evaluating). After a formalized peer review the students finally produced either new models or results using the

learned information by authoring a publishable paper (creating). (Katzlinger, Herzog, Franz, Stabauer, 2017, 2018)

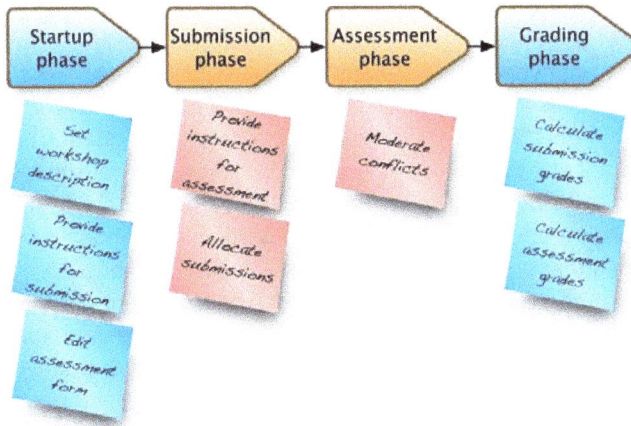

Figure 6: Virtual peer review steps, processed through Moodle's Workshop activity

We showed that the online peer review process (figure 6) increased the average student performance by 13,2%. Groups that were able to incorporate most of their feedback are also the ones that improved a lot and scored good to very good marks. Groups that did not incorporate their peers' feedback improved on average the least and are rated with average to good marks. (Katzlinger, Herzog, Franz, Stabauer, 2018)

Besides the professional knowledge, the scenario also addresses key competences according to Schaper et al, 2012 p 16f. (following Roth, 1971) that are crucial for the students' personal development and employability. According to the concept of self-competence, the students learn to take a stand regarding their individual attitude to the world, in terms of the ethical topic they have to work on, and their stance towards work, in terms of contributing to a positive working climate. They also have to reflect their personal characteristics as they are working in a team.

Naturally, this involves most of all social competence. The students develop their teamwork skills by creating a project in a virtual team and solving problems together. Even though Austria and Germany are neighbouring countries, students can still acquire intercultural skills as they notice certain differences in language, behaviour and processes. Therefore, they develop cultural awareness and expression. By working together with people from different professional backgrounds like Digital Business Management, Risk Management and Cross Media the students expand not only their network but also their interdisciplinary skills. At the same time, they improve their collaborative skills by working and writing together online with their peers. By using different virtual collaboration tools, they also enhance their digital competency. Besides communication through digital networks, the students also adopt and adapt to the different devices, applications and programs and improve their media literacy. The learning scenario also offers the students to search, critically read and interpret, evaluate and share information which helps them to enhance their information and data literacy. Just by participating in the learning scenario they are best prepared to continue learning effectively in e-Learning settings. Additionally, the learning scenario strengthens the students' methodological competency in terms of knowing how and being able to master tasks and problems in the production process of their paper. Then they are also able to process expert knowledge and are empowered to systematically work on problems and creatively combine information and potential solutions. Combing all these competencies will improve the students vocational action competence and help them to develop the necessary skills they need as successful graduates to enhance their employability (figure 7).

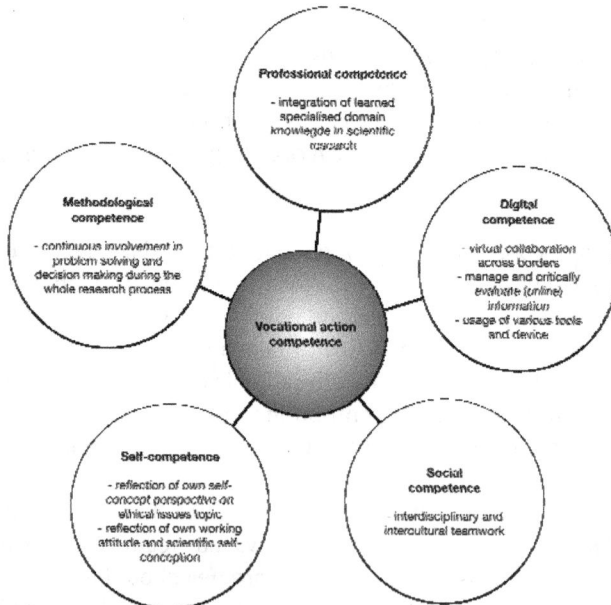

Figure 7: Competencies gained by the students /Increase in competencies in the CrossTeaching learning setting inspired by the competency framework following Schape et al, 2012 and Roth, 1971

6. Plans to further develop the initiative

Due to the high involvement of all teachers in the whole learning and research processes, a motivating learning scenario was developed that is challenging and enriching for the students as well as for the teachers. As we are constantly reflecting our teaching and reviewing students' comments and the responses of the CrossTeaching survey, we use this information to improve the learning scenario.

The student survey suggests that the learning scenario was rather received well, however, it seems that students need more guidance in the learning process. To emphasize the significance of scientific quality, we will advise the students even more about research designs, as well as the interpretation and presentation of research results. This will be done especially in the beginning of the course, but will continue in our feedback session during the semester. Furthermore, we will actively engage with the students about the outcomes of our study and show them that it helps them in their further studies and work life. We also see a potential for improvement in the peer review process. Collaborative peer feedback options, where students give feedback on feedback and evaluate the quality of the reviews is a possible way to further improve student's evaluation skills, but will need more time. If the technical improvement allows at some point the use of Natural Language Processing and Machine Learning (Ramachandran et al, 2017), it could lead to a greater efficacy of the peer review and might save time.

In an ongoing initiative we are creating a new joint online study program, targeting part time working students in Digital Business Management. This will include competency development, helping students to accomplish challenges in smart factory, data driven and robotics environments.

Overall, the adoption of technical enhancements and their use will be investigated constantly in this project, to find better blends of learning and collaboration tools for inquiry-based learning. To find out how users get the most out of technological enhancements in this learning scenario, we will establish a human behaviour laboratory where e-Learning systems use could be investigated with eye-tracking and emotion detection. As before, this research will be published to the teaching and learning community.

More information at http://crossteaching.org (new and still under construction, much of the material is still being translated).

References

Anderson, L.; Krathwohl, D. (2001) A taxonomy for learning, teaching, and assessing: A revision of Bloom's taxonomy of educational objectives, Longman, New York.

Bloom, B. S. (Ed.); Engelhart, M. D.; Furst, E. J.; Hill, W. H.; Krathwohl, D. R. (1956) Taxonomy of educational objectives: The classification of educational goals, Handbook I: Cognitive domain, David McKay Company, New York.

Herzog, M. A., Katzlinger, E, Stabauer, M. (2016) "Embedding Interuniversity Peer Review in Virtual Learning Groups. A Research-based Learning Scenario", Emerging Technologies for Education, Springer LNCS, Vol. 10108.

Katzlinger, E.; Herzog, M. A.; Franz, L., Stabauer, M. (2017) "Peer Review as a Quality Management Tool Embedded in an Inquiry-based Learning Scenario", Proceedings of 16th International Conference on Information Technology Based Higher Education and Training, ITHET2017.

Katzlinger, E.; Herzog, M. A.; Franz, L. Stabauer, M. (2018) "Reflecting Peer Reviews in Inquiry Based Learning Scenarios: An Analysis of Peer Feedback Levels and their Implementation", Proceedings of 17th International Conference on Information Technology Based Higher Education and Training, ITHET2018.

Kolb, D.; Osland, J.; Rubin, I. (1995) Organization behavior, Prince-Hall, New Jersey.

Ramachandran, L.; Gehringer, E.; Yadav, R. (2017) "Automated assessment of the quality of peer reviews using natural language processing techniques" Intl. Journal of Artificial Intelligence in Education, Jan 2017, p. 1-48.

Roth, H. (1971) Pädagogische Anthropologie: Entwicklung und Erziehung – Grundlagen einer Entwicklungspädagogik, Band 2, Schroedel, Hannover.

Schaper, N., Reis, O., Wildt, J., Horvath, E., & Bender, E. (2012) Fachgutachten zur Kompetenzorientierung in Studium und Lehre, HRK projekt nexus, pp 1-148.

Wildt, J. (2009) "Forschendes Lernen: Lernen im „Format "der Forschung", journal hochschuldidaktik, Vol 20, No. 2, pp 4-7.

Contributing Author Biographies

Elisabeth Katzlinger-Felhofer is assistant professor and deputy head of the Institute of Digital Business at the Johannes Kepler University Linz, Austria. Her research is concerned with e-learning, game-based learning, online teaching, e-tutoring and learning in virtual teams. She holds a PhD in business studies and a Master's degree in business education.

Martin Stabauer is senior scientist and deputy head of the Institute of Digital Business at the Johannes Kepler University Linz, Austria. His research revolves around technological enablers and business models of digital commerce and retail as well as around digital learning. He holds a PhD in business informatics and a Master's degree in business studies.

Leonore Franz is currently working as a research associate, and is concerned with internationalisation of teaching programs in business education. As a graduate of Public Policy she collected international experience while studying and working for non-profit organizations in Russia, Greece, Italy, Malta and Egypt. She is pursuing a PhD on strategic internationalization and governance in higher education.

Michael A. Herzog is full professor for Business Management and IT at Magdeburg-Stendal University. His research is concerned with Technology Enhanced Learning, Mobile Systems and Interaction, Simulation, and Near Field Radio Technology. He founded several international operating IT-enterprises concerning media technology and software development. Michael holds a PhD in information systems from Technische Universität Berlin.

Michael A. Herzog et al.

Interactive Pedagogical Self-study Solution for Staff Education

Sari Himanen, Hannu Järvinen, Riitta Nikkola, Anne Mäenpää, Anna Aikasalo and Anna-Liisa Karjalainen
Tampere University of Applied Sciences, Finland
sari.himanen@tamk.fi
hannu.jarvinen@tamk.fi
riitta.nikkola@tamk.fi
anne.maenpaa@tamk.fi
anna.aikasalo@tamk.fi
anna-liisa.karjalainen@tamk.fi

Abstract:
Our aim was to create a digital self-study method utilizing gamification to be used as a staff-training tool. It is possible to make the training available for the whole staff with the new mobile and interactive method. The target group of our present project is nursing staff of sheltered homes. The idea of an e-learning tool is possible to implement in any business or education sector. We have developed this application in cooperation with a Finnish ICT organisation. The application is in the internet and used by computer and mobile device. An essential point of our idea is its pedagogical solution. Our aim was to plan the self-study method to have a strongly interactive operational logic which requires activeness from the learner and stimulates the learner's learning. We have created 12 different modules to the platform, each of which takes about four hours to be studied and consists of 24 parts. Every module starts with tests that measure the attitude to and pre-competence on the topic. These tests stimulate learners' motivation to study the subject. The following 20 study-parts include text, photos, videos, short tests or questions to be reflected during the next phase. Each of the parts takes about 10 minutes. The idea of this structure is continuing learning. You can study one or two parts a day, you can reflect on the studied topics at your work and assimilate new information better. The part 23 is a self-evaluation section; learners can evaluate and reflect on their learning. The last part is the final exam. Learning results can be analysed by comparing the results of the pre-study test and final exam. The learners earn points during the module and good performance is rewarded with a gold, silver or bronze medal.

1. Introduction

Our aim was to create a digital self-study method to be used as a staff-training tool in sheltered homes for elderly people. It is possible to make the training available for the whole staff with the new mobile and interactive self-study method without the need for them to be absent from work.

The further education aims at maintaining and developing professional skills. According to research, professional further education can improve effectiveness, service quality and client satisfaction in health care as well as promote staff's commitment to work and job satisfaction (Finnish Ministry of Social Affairs and Health 2004).

The target group of our present project is nursing staff in Finland but the idea of an e-learning tool is possible to implement in any business or education sector. You just have to input your substance content to the platform.

The interactive pedagogical self-study solution for staff training, called Palko, is developed in an EU-funded project. The project has four main objectives and measures:

1. To plan a mobile pedagogical solution in cooperation with an ICT organisation.
2. To support nursing staff's competence, occupational wellbeing and empowering by focusing the training on key everyday knowledge and skills.
3. To plan the self-study method to have a strongly interactive operational logic which requires activeness from the learner and stimulates the learner's learning.
4. The final objective is to improve the quality of nursing situation interaction experienced by elderly people, increase their trust in staff, and strengthen their functional ability and sense of safety.

The two-year (2017-2019) project's measures respond to the four main objectives.

1. Coding of the pedagogical ICT solution was purchased from a Finnish ICT organisation.
2. The contents of the staff education were planned based on literature and study findings. Twelve professional nursing topics were chosen and the study modules were produced.
3. A pedagogical solution was planned and tested. The written learning material was made applicable for mobile devices, including the reflective approach and interactive user interface.

4. The ready product was implemented for the use of approximately 200 nursing staff members in spring 2018 and its functioning and impact will be evaluated in December 2018.

2. The infrastructure

Project team
The idea of the pedagogical solution was designed by the project team. Members of the team are staff of Tampere University of Applied Sciences; 4 nursing lecturers, physiotherapy lecturer, Senior Systems Analyst, and project coordinator. Coding of the technical solution was purchased from a Finnish ICT organisation, JJ-Net Group Oy.

Pedagogical solution
An essential point of our idea is its pedagogical solution. Our aim was to plan the self-study method to have a strongly interactive operational logic which requires activeness from the learner and stimulates the learner's learning. The planned application is based on continuous reflection, i.e. repeated evaluation of personal competence, understanding of personal learning, and guidance. New knowledge is constructed reflecting on prior knowledge. (Rauste-von Wright & von Wright 1994.)

Topics of the staff education
We have created 12 study modules (Figure 1). Topics of the modules are based on literature and the findings of focus group surveys and interviews, which were performed at the beginning of the project.

Safe implementation of pharmacotherapy
Professional interaction and challenging situations
Functional ability from rehabilitation
Nutrition as basis for wellbeing
Most common diseases and their treatment
Basics of aseptic work and treatment of chronic wounds
Client-oriented daily basic care
Evaluation of health changes and practices in acute situations
Treatment at final stages of life
Coping at work and occupational wellbeing
Memory loss diseases and mental health promotion
Registration and use of client information

Figure 1: Topics of the study modules

Structure of the study modules

Each of the modules has the same structure (table 1) and each of them takes about four hours to be completed. They consist of 24 parts.

Table 1: Structure of the study modules

Part 1	Attitude test (to stimulate and motivate learning of the topic)
Part 2	Pre-competence test (to indicate knowledge)
Parts 3-22	Study parts
Part 23	Self-evaluation test (the learner can evaluate his/her learning)
Part 24	Final exam (same questions as in the pre-competence test

Each of the parts (3-22) takes about 10 minutes to complete. They include short texts, photos, videos, short tests or questions to be reflected during the next phase. The idea of this structure is continuing learning. You can study one or two parts a day, you can reflect on the studied topics at your work, and assimilate new information better.

Hardware/software

The learning environment works as an information-secure cloud service on servers maintained and administered by the supplier (JJ-Net Group Oy) in Finland. Administration of learning materials and studying in the environment are easy on computer and all modern mobile devices – it is enough to have an internet connection and up-to-date web browser.

The learning environment has been built on a platform whose tools make it possible to produce pedagogical contents without coding skills. The contents are built as study modules. Materials/contents are attached to the modules by saving them on a form. The form has ready fields for images and videos, texts, questions and responses. There are several task types. Images are attached to the task pages by embedding and videos are linked for example from YouTube. It is possible to define whether answering to questions gives points or not. The ready material is published by clicking Publish.

Users can see in real time how they have progressed in completing the study module and how many points they have earned. The system has limits for gold, silver and bronze medals. The system shows how the person's competence has developed when the pre-competence test and final exam results are compared with one another.

The learning environment is protected and requires login. The sheltered home using the environment can be in charge of its user administration or outsource the service to the system supplier. Only the person's name and email address are needed to create the username. The system sends the created username to the given email address. Persons who have administrator rights in the sheltered home (for example superiors) can follow users' (employees') performance and competence development.

3. The challenges

One essential challenge in our development process was how to create a platform which is interactive, fun and useful. Gamification could be an answer but not easy to put into practice.

In games the learning process can be divided into elements in which learning takes place by cognitive knowledge building during the game functions. Integration of visual learning situations from real-life working life into the contents can increase interest in studying and the learning environment. (Michael & Chan 2006, deFreitas & Jarvis 2007, Kiili 2007.)

Even if the Palko application is not a typical game, we aim at creating addictive game features through collection of points and pursue of medals. The challenge was to make meaningful questions to map competence and earn points but at the same time to support reflection by encouraging users to consider the learnt in relation to their work.

We aimed at strengthening the authenticity of the learning environment by integrating many photographs and videos on real working life situations into the contents. We took some photographs by ourselves and purchased others from image banks. It was laborious but fun to make the videos. We screenwrote, acted and shot the videos. Media students helped us in editing.

The learning experience often becomes deeper when the learning environment includes activities that require the user's contribution. If the learning environment gives feedback, it can support reflective thinking and knowledge construction on the learnt matter. (Kiili 2007, Rieber & Noah 2008.)

Palko study modules always consist of 24 parts, each of which takes about 10 minutes to complete. Every part has elements which require activeness from the user. The parts are independent. It is possible to complete them gradually in which case knowledge is constructed gradually. The challenge has been to scale the contents in such a way that every module consists of 24 x 10 minutes.

Games can be planned to emphasise individuals' competence development or knowledge construction in cooperation (Kiili 2007). The Palko application aims at supporting both of these. Questions that support reflection challenge users to consider their working methods and discuss matters in the work community. When several work community members study the same contents almost at the same time, it can be possible to develop the operating culture in the work community. Implementation of new practices is often challenging and requires that all work community members share the same will.

No learning environment guarantees learning but a good learning environment can support and encourage students in their learning process. We have tried to create a new learning environment in which studying takes place gradually alongside work and in which the learnt matters can continuously be reflected on the work. It is interesting to study later if the method produces learning which can also be seen as a change in nurses' practical work. This will be studied by means of resident interviews.

For us Palko developers the process has also been a learning process. New technology has required learning by trial and error. The ICT software supplier has answered to our technical questions immediately or on the same day, either by telephone or email. This has enabled introduction of diverse technical solutions. Clear work distribution between the project team members has helped in working on the entity. The project team has met every two weeks and between the meetings the team members have worked independently on the contents.

In order to increase use of games in education, we need a growing number of teachers who recognise games as an important media and are interested in using them in education (Van Eck 2006, Kuusisto 2014). We five health care teachers belong to this group. We have together solved pedagogical, contentual and even technical questions.

4. How the initiative was received

First test among students
In October 2017, 13 first-year nursing students tested the application and evaluated its four first modules. The students studied all the parts and wrote an evaluation report of 10-15 pages in accordance with the given instructions.

The students evaluated the contents interesting, they considered the visual presentation manner meaningful, and use of the application fluent. They experienced the contents useful from the viewpoint of working life.

There were tests at the beginning of each study module. The attitude test asked how important respondents considered the asked matters and how they usually behaved in the situations. The competence test measured initial competence on the topic before the independent study. The purpose of the initial test part is to rouse the users' interest in studying the topic and reflecting on their work. Most students understood the pedagogical thought of the learning environment: "The initial questions called my attention to practices and personal experiences as a nurse."

Each study module takes about four hours and consists of 10-minute independent parts. The students understood this pedagogical idea well: "It is good that you can interrupt completing the parts and continue them later. It is easier to concentrate if you only do a couple of parts at a time."

The parts consisted of text, images, videos, questions and consideration tasks. This diverse material was praised by students: "I would be pleased to complete the education in this form, especially when the parts can be continued later. Learning in this way is meaningful especially in parts where you can respond yourself and think about questions. "

There was a competence test at the end of the study module. It measured competence on the matters covered by the material. Points and a medal were given on the test. The test was considered meaningful and encouraging: "The final test was nice and it gave a feeling of success when you remembered the matters well."

Students received medals on the study module based on their competence. Most gold medals (7) were received on the wellbeing from nutrition module. Pharmacotherapy appeared to be the most difficult module with no gold medals.

Test among practical nurses

In autumn 2017 Palko was tested by 7 practical nurses in sheltered homes. They studied the four study modules which were ready. They were interviewed and the data were analysed based on the interview themes. The themes were contents, meaningfulness of tasks, operational logic, and student experience.

Contents and meaningfulness of tasks

The interviewees experienced the Palko learning environment contents interesting and useful. The contents were considered appropriately demanding even if the pharmacotherapy module was experienced difficult: "It is good that it is not too easy. It was quite challenging."

More new information was yearned for in some parts but repetition of familiar matters was also experienced good. It helped to combine information with practical work in a new way and change some practices. Some interviewees considered they gained new viewpoints into their work, especially in the nutrition module which also induced them to consider the work community practices in implementing clients' nutrition.

The interaction part was liked and it contained interesting matters in the interviewees' opinion. The examples and consideration tasks induced the interviewees to evaluate their work and take on new viewpoints: "Practices have changed completely. And still improved further."

The interviewees found the content presentation mainly good and appropriately varied. Videos were considered as an especially good presentation manner and they were remembered best. Particularly the realistic rehabilitation videos were thanked for: "All these reminders and instructions were worth their weight in gold".

Some interviewees told that they had noticed increase in client satisfaction when the learnt was used in practical nursing.

Operational logic

Most study module texts were experienced to be of an appropriate length, only a few were found too long. Division into sections and repetition parts were hoped for in the long texts.

Long texts were experienced difficult to remember if there were few questions between.

The questions and consideration tasks of the parts were much liked. They stop the person to consider matters and even more of them were yearned for. Clearer instructions were hoped for writing numerical answers.

Images and videos were praised as extremely good. Some interviewees had however difficulties in opening the videos or opening tables in a larger size to read their contents. Usability problems were related to different computers, operating systems, or internet browsers. When the available network was slow, for example in trains, opening of sites was slow and use of the software troublesome. The interviewees liked the fact that the study modules were divided in parts. This made it possible to complete one part at a time and continue later. The final exam was considered good as it told users how much information they had learnt. Three interviewees mentioned the computer as the best way to use the learning environment. One thought that the tablet was the best and another that the computer and tablet were equally good.

Student experience
The studying experience was seen as being fun. The digital method was considered good and easy. The independent way of studying was liked, independent reading helped to learn. As it was about further education for staff, the interviewees considered it important to be able to use working hours for the studies. Two interviewees described that they had willingness to learn, which increased their motivation to study. Concentration was at times experienced difficult along with work and it was difficult to find time for studying. Due to lack of time and hustle and bustle at the workplace, studying often took place at home and in the night shift.

Summary
The developed further education method received a positive welcome. Digital self-study implementation as parts was experienced meaningful and learning supporting. Interactivity and the reflective method were thanked for and according to the feedback they encouraged to consider personal practices and even change them. Independent studying however takes time, which the employer should take into consideration.

Based on the received feedback, corrections were made into the application contents, implementation manner, and technique. Testing will continue by the end of 2018 and changes will be made as defects and needs arise.

5. The learning outcomes
The application has an integrated function which compares the pre-competence test and final exam results. It makes it possible to evaluate the impact of the learning material, i.e. strengthening of competence. The enclosed table describes students' and nurses' results in the six study modules. The results cover the

period of time until August. Based on the data it can be stated that all users learnt. Students' pre-competence was weaker than nurses' and they learnt more by means of Palko, in the other study modules except the Final stages of life module. In the competence tests, the learning results improved on average by approximately 15 percent in the four study modules (12,4 % – 17,5 %) and approximately 7 percent in other two modules (6,5 % - 7,7 %). The Rehabilitation module results improved most, by 17,5 percent on average. (Table 2.)

Table 2: Competence growth between the pre-competence test and final exam among passed and failed students and nurses.

	Accepted (70% right)	Fail (under 70% right)	In total Average growth
Pharmacotherapy			
Student (n)	8	5	13
Competence growth	29.4%	14.0%	23.5%
Nurse (n)	46	2	48
Competence growth	12.9%	10%	12.6%
Professional interaction			
Student (n)	11	2	13
Competence growth	26.1%	8.5%	24.1%%
Nurse (n)	51	4	55
Competence growth	12.2%	11.8%	12.2%
Nutrition			
Student (n)	12	1	13
Competence growth	22.9%	-7.0%	20.6%
Nurse (n)	24	0	24
Competence growth	8.0%		8.0%
Rehabilitation			
Student (n)	13	1	14
Competence growth	21.3%	3.0%	20.0%
Nurse (n)	19	3	22
Competence growth	13.5%	31.0%	15.9%
Aseptic work			
Student (n)	4	3	7
Competence growth	19.0%	1.0%	11.3%
Nurse (n)	19	3	22
Competence growth	6.6%	6.7%	6.6%
Final stages of life			
Student (n)	4	3	7
Competence growth	11.0%	-3.3%	4.9%
Nurse (n)	27	3	30
Competence growth	8.2%	-4.7%	6.9%

6. Plans to further develop the initiative
Use of the application continues in five sheltered homes until the end of the year. There are more than 200 users. The users have the possibility to give continuous

feedback if they notice any content or technical defects in the study modules. The aim is to correct the defects immediately. At the end of the year, user feedback will be collected on student experiences. Marketing and distribution of the application will be started during the final part of the year. Based on the initial results, the application appears to increase users' competence and thus be effective. The aim is to create a self-study material for superiors on the same platform next year. The platform can be used in any field of study in future.

References

Finnish Ministry of Social Affairs and Health, 2004. Terveydenhuollon täydennyskoulutussuositus. Helsinki: Sosiaali- ja terveysministeriön oppaita 3. [online] Available at http://urn.fi/URN:NBN:fi-fe201504227148

de Freitas, S. and Jarvis, S., 2007. Serious Games – Engaging Training Solutions: A Research and Development Project for Supporting Training Needs. British Journal of Educational Technology 38(3), pp.523-525.

Kiili, K., 2007. Foundation for problem-based gaming. British Journal of Educational Technology 38(3), pp.394-404.

Kuusisto, K., 2014. Hyöty ja huvi – kaupallisten pelien anti opetuspeleihin. Pelitutkimuksen vuosikirja 2014, pp.88-96.

Michael, D. and Chen, S., 2006. Serious Games: Games that Educate, Train and Inform. Boston, MA: Thomson.

Rauste-von Wright, M. and von Wright, J., 1994/2003. Learning and education. Porvoo-Helsinki-Juva: WSOY.

Rieber, L. and Noah, D., 2008. Games, simulations, and visual metaphors in education: antagonism between enjoyment and learning. Educational Media International, 45(2), pp.77-92.

Van Eck, R., 2006. Digital Game-Based Learning: It's Not Just the Digital Natives Who Are Restless. Educause 41(2), pp.16-30.

Contributing Author Biographies:

Sari Himanen works as a senior lecturer in Tampere University of Applied Sciences. She completed her PhD in Education from University of Tampere. She has 16 years of experience in nursing teaching. She has developed diverse ICT-based teaching methods in nursing education and studied their effects on learning.

Riitta Nikkola, PhD, is a senior lecturer at Tampere University of Applied Sciences. She has a BS in medical-surgical nursing and MS in nursing education. Her 2013 dissertation explored osteoarthritis in elderly patients. With 23 years teaching nursing, she has written about medication calculation in nursing textbooks. Her interests are asepsis and medication.

Anna-Liisa Karjalainen is a senior system analyst in Tampere University of Applied Sciences. She works as a project manager in a variety of ICT-projects and has taught information technology for nursing students. She has many years of experience in supporting development of teaching. She has cooperated with lecturers to improve diverse ICT-based teaching methods.

Hannu Järvinen, MSc, senior lecturer (physiotherapy) at Tampere University of Applied Sciences. He has 10 years of experience in physiotherapy teaching, especially physiotherapy for the elderly and neurological rehabilitation.

Anna Aikasalo has worked as a teacher in Tampere University of Applied Sciences since 2015. Prior to teaching she worked as a nurse in various fields of health care. Anna completed her master's degree in Health Sciences from University of Tampere in 2016. Her master's thesis explored digital health education.

Anne Mäenpää (RN, M.Sc) is a senior lecturer, in Degree Programme in Nursing and Health Care at Tampere University of Applied Sciences. She has many years of experience developing ICT-based teaching methods in nursing education and she was a part of a group developing a digital learning game for nursing students to practice delivering babies.

MR-supported Voice Training for Lecturers of Large Classes

Using a Virtual Voice Training Environment to Bring Large Lecture Halls Into Small Seminar Rooms

Kathrin Hohlbaum, Valerie Stehling, Max Haberstroh and Ingrid Isenhardt

Cybernetics Lab IMA & IfU, RWTH Aachen University, Germany

kathrin.hohlbaum@ima-ifu.rwth-aachen.de

Abstract

Although their voice is one of their most important tools for conveying information, many lecturers lack knowledge about the proper and effective use of it. In order to prevent chronic voice problems or even occupational incapacity, many universities offer voice trainings. However, often the settings in which such trainings take place are not representative of the actual work environment. This gap is being addressed within the cooperative project "ELLI 2" – Excellent Teaching and Learning in Engineering Science, funded by the German Federal Ministry of Education and Research (BMBF). Within this project, the innovative Mixed Reality supported Voice Training provides lecturers with the opportunity to train their voices in a virtual setting that is both an acoustic and visual realistic simulation of their everyday teaching environment. This is attained by integrating a specially developed Virtual Voice Training Environment (VVTE) in the context of a voice seminar. The latest prototype of the VVTE comprises six different rooms of various sizes. To generate these settings, visual and acoustic data from real lecture halls have been integrated into a Mixed Reality environment. The participants can immerse into this environment by the use of VR glasses, headphones and a microphone. While the participants apply the methods learned in a safe and realistic virtual environment, they are guided and provided with direct feedback by a professional voice trainer. The implementation of the VVTE into a voice training seminar will be thoroughly evaluated and constantly adjusted towards the needs of all parties involved. In the future, the open source VVTE will be applicable to other universities and in further contexts, e.g. therapeutic uses or a Mixed Reality supported teacher education.

1. Introduction

For lecturers, especially for those who teach large classes, their voice is one of the most important tools for conveying information. Nevertheless, a considerate use of their voice poses an often underestimated challenge for lecturers. A permanent

Kathrin Hohlbaum et al.

incorrect use of the voice can result in chronic voice impairments, possibly even leading to occupational incapacity. For this reason, many universities offer voice trainings in which lecturers can train to use their voice correctly. The environment of those trainings, however, often does not provide a great resemblance of the actual conditions in large lecture halls and side effects in terms of noise and other disruptions. Based on the assumption that Mixed-Reality (MR) technologies can provide close-to-realistic experiences in areas where the real-world learning or teaching environment is not available, a MR-Voice Lab has been developed to provide a realistic simulation of a lecturer's teaching environment.

The MR-supported Voice Training for Lecturers of Large Classes is part of the cooperative project "ELLI 2" – Excellent Teaching and Learning in Engineering Science. This project is funded by the German Federal Ministry of Education and Research (BMBF). As part of this project, researchers at TU Dortmund, Ruhr Universität Bochum und RWTH Aachen University are working together, pursuing the common goal to continuously improve teaching quality and studying conditions in engineering education. As a part of the ELLI project, the MR-supported Voice Training enriches classical voice seminars with the possibility to train the highly strained voices of lecturers in realistic virtual environments.

Based on visual and acoustic data from several real lecture halls, a range of mixed reality scenarios have been created. With the help of the software RAVEN (Schröder & Vorländer, 2011), various acoustic scenarios, such as different levels of background noise can be simulated. At RWTH Aachen University, the MR-Voice Lab is integrated into a professional voice training seminar for lecturers to allow participants to train the use of their voice in an acoustically and visually accurate, highly immersive scenario. The seminar is oriented towards Kolb's (Kolb & Kolb, 2005) experiential learning cycle and will cover various topics, e.g. information on how the voice is produced and which factors such as breathing, posture and tension can have an influence. Voice trainings usually consist of a lot of practical exercises, e.g. on posture, tension and relaxation, respiration exercises and exercises on phonation and resonance (Pizolato et al., 2013). In addition, a common practice in voice treatment or damage prevention is the use of imagination. Often the imagination of a large, reverberating room is used to promote the voice's resonance (Hering, 2010). Guided by a professional voice coach, the seminar is going to comprise all the above-mentioned topics and exercises, supplemented by the MR-Voice Lab. Particularly concerning the practical exercises and the use of imaginary aids, the MR-Voice Lab represents a unique extension of the existing possibilities.

2. The infrastructure

For the development of the MR-Voice Lab, Unreal Engine is used. This software environment provides a toolset for creating virtual surroundings. In order to simulate the spatial characteristics of a room, it is captured visually with a 360° camera. In addition to the spatial representation, the reverberation of the respective room is simulated and added to the simulation. For this purpose, the convolution reverb algorithm is used. Supported by the Institute for Technical Acoustics of the RWTH Aachen University, the real-time room acoustics simulation framework RAVEN is used to calculate a room's impulse response. By help of this software it is possible to simulate room acoustics based on estimations or on detailed information on the room's characteristics. It allows the realistic reproduction of the sound field and the alteration of the acoustic properties of a room. This way, different acoustic scenarios, e.g. different levels of background noise within a lecture hall, can be simulated. Subsequently, the convolution reverb algorithm calculates an approximate echo of the participant's voice in the respective environment from the simulated impulse response. The software Ableton Live is used to provide users with a low and therefore realistic response time of their own reverberated voice. The MR-Voice Lab is made available for a Head Mounted Display (HMD), e.g. the Oculus Rift Consumer Version One (Figure 1).

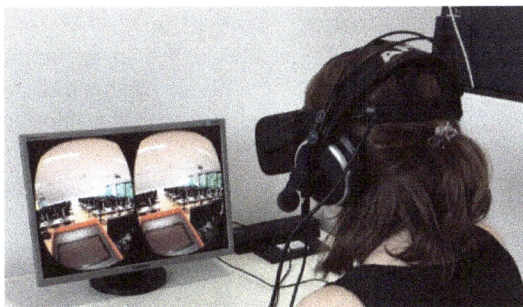

Figure 10 Setup of the MR-Voice Lab

This allows users to look around freely to obtain a visual impression of the room. The voice of the speaker is fed into the system via a microphone, reverberated according to the acoustic properties of the simulated room and transmitted back to the speaker via headphones. The latest version of the MR-Voice Lab is provided open source3 and can be downloaded and implemented into training by anyone.

---

[3] https://github.com/Cybernetics-Lab-Aachen/Mixed-Reality-Voice-Training

3. The challenges

The first challenge that had to be overcome was to put the initial theoretical idea of developing an MR-supported voice training into practice. The technical feasibility of this project was demonstrated with the development of the MR-Voice Lab. In addition, a professional voice trainer had to be found who showed interest and willingness to use the developed technique in a seminar. Finding a professional voice and rhetoric trainer who already used the MR-Voice Lab during a pilot seminar, this challenge was overcome as well. Furthermore, during this first trial run of the seminar, meaningful application possibilities of MR.-Voice Labs were identified.

Visualizing students inside the, yet empty, lecture halls is a highly requested and desired feature. This can be done by either integrating recordings of real students or by integrating virtual students into the simulation. Nevertheless, these ideas involve various challenges that have to be considered: If real students were to be recorded, only a limited extent of possible scenarios could be realized. Reactions of the recorded students could not be altered and therefore adapted to a specific training situation or to visually simulate different room occupancy rates. By integrating virtual students instead of real students, their reactions could be altered, matching the respective acoustic scenario. Implementing such a virtual crowd that is able to react to the lecturer is by far the most difficult, yet the most exciting challenge for the further development of the MR-Voice Lab. To realize this idea, all lecture halls must be reconstructed three-dimensionally and the virtual students have to be created. Since the fully virtualized reconstruction and the modelling and programming of virtual students is a time-consuming matter, an interim solution was proposed: Colored markers that serve as visual anchor points the user can focus on while speaking (Figure 2). Those have already been implemented into two of the scenarios.

Figure 11: Lecture hall provided with colored markers as visual anchor points

4. How the initiative was received

An iterative approach is used to successively expand the features of the MR-Voice Lab and to improve and realize its integration into a voice training seminar. As of today, feedback on the MR-Voice Lab was obtained through tests with experts and through short interviews with stakeholders from the fields of professional voice coaching and software engineering. Further feedback from experts in didactics as well as from representatives of various industries was obtained at trade fairs, conferences and presentations during workshops. Also, the concept of the Mixed Reality-supported Voice training was presented at the Culture and Computer Science Conference 2018 in Berlin and the LEARNTEC trade fair in Karlsruhe, Germany. At LEARNTEC the initiative was awarded the bitcom innovation prize for digital education (delina) in higher education. Overall, on all these occasions the project was always met with great interest and a need for such an initiative was expressed both by representatives from the fields of education as well as from industry. Finally, in June 2018 a pilot voice training seminar that integrated the MR-Voice Lab was held. The participants of this seminar have expressed their enthusiasm about the opportunity to test their voice in such a realistic environment. Nevertheless, they expressed the wish to have visually and acoustically integrated virtual students into the environment.

This is an important matter on which intensive work will be carried out in the upcoming months.

5. The learning outcomes

Schuster (2015) showed that an immersive hardware such as e.g. the Occulus Rift can lead to higher spatial presence. Nevertheless, possible distractions due to e.g. the device's unfamiliarity or discomfort may occur (Janßen, 2018). Due to these reported experiences, the seminar contains episodes in which the MR-Voice Lab is introduced gently by using it in short exercises episodes. Additionally, feedback concerning the participant's emotions while using the MR-Voice Lab will be obtained and incorporated into the continuous development of the seminar.

During the pilot seminar, all five participants reported a high spatial presence, none of them suffered from motion sickness. The development, implementation and evaluation of this initiative deals with the learning aspect of MR as a tool for imparting knowledge and skills. Therefore, over the course of the project, the MR-Voice Lab will pass through several pre-tests as well as optimization phases and formative evaluations.

6. Plans to further develop the initiative

Over the course of the project ELLI 2 MR-Voice Lab will be expanded by adding further lecture halls and seminar rooms, e.g. those of the project partner Ruhr Universität Bochum (RUB). The integration of the measurement and simulation data will allow for further acoustic alterations such as varying e.g. the level of background noise. At this point, the visual impression of the captured rooms still needs to be improved in terms of simulating different visual scenarios of crowdedness (empty/half-full/full room). Different approaches to the implementation of this goal will be tested and applied in the further course of the project. Also, the implementation of the MR-Voice Lab into a Voice Training will be thoroughly evaluated and constantly adjusted towards the needs of the participants and the trainers. The development, implementation and evaluation of the MR-Voice Lab into a voice training not only helps to prevent chronic voice impairments and thereby improve the quality of lectures given in large lecture halls. It also contributes to answering the research question whether MR constitutes a reasonable addition to classical voice trainings. Furthermore, it also deals with the learning aspect of MR as a tool for transferring knowledge and skills. Besides questions regarding the promotion of the participant's learning processes, the question whether MR constitutes a reasonable addition to classical voice trainings as well as technical challenges are to be considered for the further development of the MR-Voice Lab. This includes a number of research questions, such as: How the learning process of the participants can be fostered while using the MR-Voice Lab. What differences can be identified between a traditional and a MR-supported training? Is a transfer of acquired skills facilitated by the use of the MR-Voice Lab? How can trainer and participants interact in the MR setting? How must the trainer be instructed to efficiently use the application in voice training? Moreover, it is to be investigated in which contexts beyond higher education such MR scenarios can be applied. Furthermore, since it is provided open source, the MR-Voice Lab is deployable to other universities and in further contexts e.g. therapeutic uses or teacher education.

References

Hering, G. (2010). Die Wirkung von Vorstellungshilfen auf die Sprechstimme. Forum Logopadie, 24 (4).

Janßen, D. (2018). Einfluss von Persönlichkeitseigenschaften und immersiven Benutzerschnittstellen auf User Experience und Leistung. Dissertation, RWTH Aachen University. Apprimus Verlag, Aachen

Kolb, A. Y., & Kolb, D. A. (2005). Learning styles and learning spaces: Enhancing experiential learning in higher education. Academy of management learning & education, 4(2), pp.193-212.

Pizolato, R., Rehder, M., de Castro Meneghim, M., Ambrosano, G., Mialhe, F., & Pereira, A. (2013). Impact on quality of life in teachers after educational actions for prevention of voice disorders: a longitudinal study. Health and quality of life outcomes, 11(1), 28

Schröder, D. & Vorländer, M. (2011). RAVEN: A real-time framework for the auralization of interactive virtual environments. In Forum Acusticum, pp 1541-1546. Denmark: Aalborg.

Schuster, K. (2015). Einfluss natürlicher Benutzerschnittstellen zur Steuerung des Sichtfeldes und der Fortbewegung auf Rezeptionsprozesse in virtuellen Lernumgebungen. Tectum Verlag.

Author Biography

Kathrin Hohlbaum is a scientific researcher in the research group Digital Learning Environments at the interdisciplinary Institute for Information Management in Mechanical Engineering (IMA) at RWTH Aachen University in Germany. The core areas of her activities cover the fields of communication, education and digitalization.

Digest: Digital Method for Self and Peer Assessment of Exercises in Mathematics and Statistics University Studies

Mika Koskenoja, Toni Lehtonen, Aku Leivonen, Joonas Nuutinen, Petteri Piiroinen, Nea Rantanen and Sirkka-Liisa Varvio
University of Helsinki, Department of Mathematics and Statistics, Finland
mika.koskenoja@helsinki.fi
toni.lehtonen@helsinki.fi
aku.leivonen@helsinki.fi
joonas.nuutinen@helsinki.fi
petteri.piiroinen@helsinki.fi
nea.rantanen@helsinki.fi
sirkka-liisa.varvio@helsinki.fi

Abstract
DIgest is a collaborative e-learning environment based on self- and peer assessment of exercises in mathematics and statistics studies at the University of Helsinki and, in parallel, at the Open University. DIgest method takes into account and fosters different studying and learning techniques. Weekly exercises are published in Moodle where a digital forum is available for students' and instructors' discussion while working for solutions. After the deadline for submissions, the model solutions are published. The students self-assess their own solutions and peer assess solutions of two other anonymous students using these model solutions together with precise grading instructions. The scoring system gives points on the basis of the quality of solutions, and also from the process of performing the assessment process. In case that the three scores differ more than a certain criterium, the instructor makes an assessment too. Time devoted to the rechecking process has been considerably diminished by implementing scripts. These scripts visualize the cases that need inspection and re-evaluation by highlighting them with color-codes. In addition, we have improved the Moodle's default of scoring. All these scripts have been written in Clojure programming language and they were compiled with ClojureScript to JavaScript programs that modify the behaviour of the Moodle. Because of the nature of statistics and mathematics, the most important aspect of a solution is the description how to get there, i.e. the presented path to the solution. A presented solution can be worth maximum points, even if the final numerical answer is not correct. Fortunately, the students seem to understand this, and questions – as well as answers from teaching assistants – during the peer and self assessment stage usually clarify the complications. The DIgest method offers

effective reflection: every student explores his/her own solutions, two other students' solutions and the model solutions. This means that a student sees several different correct and incorrect solutions which implies more and deeper learning. Students practice many important everyday skills like giving and receiving feedback, both positive and negative. Student feedback of the DIGest method has been very positive so that 80-85% of students love the method, and only 1-2% hate it. We have clear evidence that the understanding of mathematics and statistics is better than before when using traditional exercise methods. In addition, the number of course completions has increased. In future, we shall produce short video clips introducing the main concepts of the courses. This allows students to follow the courses at home; not even following the lectures necessities the travelling to the science campus. R-programming is a central tool in bachelor level statistics courses. In future, this part will be improved, as a considerable amount of R-exercises can be assessed automatically with the Test My Code (TMC) system of the Computer Science Department in a collaborative basis.

1. Introduction

DIGest is a flexible and collaborative method for organizing e-learning by self- and peer assessment of exercises in mathematics and statistics studies at the University of Helsinki (UH) and, in parallel, at the Open University of UH. Our general mission is the importance of self- and peer assessment which are known to enhance teaching and learning effectiveness by helping the students to develop their reflective and critical thinking skills, as well as their self-confidence as learners. A digital environment permitting these positive outcomes, i.e. an e-learning environment, has the additional practical advantages of allowing learning and teaching independent of time and space - with the exception of deadlines. We have modified some Moodle learning management system features by using programs generated with ClojureScript so that the system meets our purposes.

Typically, mathematics and statistics exercises are solved with "pen and paper" or they are computer based (like programming) and in statistics also short essays. Traditionally there have been weekly exercise group meetings where the students present their solutions to other students and an instructor controls activities. However, this is not time efficient for the students and not cost efficient for the institutions. Both mathematics and statistics are important or even compulsory minors for other disciplines. The campus structure of UH comprises four campuses, several kilometers apart from each other.

DIGest is an atmosphere enabling collaborative learning and teaching of mathematics and statistics in UH. Weekly exercises are published in Moodle learning management system where a digital forum is available for students' and instructors' discussions while working for solutions. After the deadline of submissions, the model solutions of exercises are published and based on them with precise instructions the students self-assess their own solutions and peer assess solutions of two other students. This process is finally strictly supervised by course teachers. DIGest guarantees that every student receives feedback from his/her all exercise solutions proving a simple tool for formative assessment. DIGest method takes into account and fosters different studying and learning techniques.

2. The infrastructure

Usually 350–600 students participate in bachelor level mathematics and statistics courses in UH. The responsible teacher for a given course is typically a university lecturer who is the leader of a team consisting of 5-8 teaching assistants. Teaching assistants are usually master level students. Authors of this work, Mika Koskenoja, Petteri Piiroinen, Sirkka-Liisa Varvio, are university lecturers and Toni Lehtonen, Aku Leivonen, Joonas Nuutinen, Nea Rantanen are teaching assistants, comprising the core DIGest-team.

The weekly exercise set in a typical course consists of 8 exercises (range 6-10). Weekly exercises are published in the weekly Moodle-area. One week is given for solving the exercises and communications - questions and answers - in the weekly discussion area. The general rule is that students give help to each other and teaching assistants contribute if needed. Forwarding correct answers is not allowed. When the submission area is closed (submission deadline), Moodle delivers two anonymous exercise sets to each student and she/he will also get own solutions for evaluation. The document comprising correct answers, with instructions for giving scores, is also published. The most effective and unequivocal scoring system is the following. A correct solution is worth of 2 points, a solution with reasonable correct elements is 1 point, and no answer, or totally wrong solution is 0 points. Thus, a student can get from 8 weekly exercises maximum of 16 points. While evaluating the answers, the student has to provide a written rationale for giving less than 2 points.

The student also gets points from performing the peer and self-assessments: 2 points from each assessment (one self-assessment and two peer assessments). Therefore, the maximum weekly score is 22 points in this example. In the courses with more than 8 weekly exercises, say 10 exercises, the weight of a self-assessment and a peer assessment is raised by giving 3 points per assessment, instead of 2 points.

Let's consider this with an imaginary example. From one weekly exercise set a given student self-assess his/her solutions with 16 points. She/he also is given 16 points from one peer reviewing student, but only 12 points from the other peer reviewing student. The situation will not be left as is. A teaching assistant also evaluates the solutions and gives points. Let's consider another example. A student gets 15 points from a self-assessment, but he/she has not received any peer assessments. This can happen, since not all students in every week perform the process. In this case, the points from a teaching assistant are also needed. In general, teaching assistants inspect all those cases in which more than 2-point discrepancy in the points is revealed. After this inspection process, points from weekly exercises are published.

Although the process is under a strict control of teachers and teaching assistants, there might be doubts that other students (peer review) have an impact to final course grade. DIGest is equipped with a "satisfaction guarantee". The weekly exercise points have an effect on the course grade, the impact is between 30% - 100% (no exam). Since the DIGest scores are given by peers and students themselves, some scores may look suspicious, even though the course instructors have checked the results. Doubts and unhappiness are not acceptable. After the final course grades are published, the so-called complaint box is opened. In the complaint box he students may leave well justified reclamations to re-evaluate their exercises if they believe that some scores should be different from those she/he has finally received. The re-evaluation is done by the course instructors (not peers) and only in the case that there is a possibility that the course grade could improve. On average 0-5 students per course send a reclamation, indicating that the system is fair and works really well.

3. The challenges
One of the major challenges is the allocation of (unnecessary) time for taking care of the process. The points from self-assessments and peer assessments need to be under the control of teachers, and we use certain criteria for the differences between the 3 points that a given student receives. In addition, there are also students that do not perform the assessment process.

How to minimize the time that teaching assistants need to devote for checking and correcting the results before publishing the weekly results? For example, in the course Probability calculus I in 2017, there were 312 submissions per week on the average. Out of all those students who submitted their exercises 90 % in the average submitted also the self- and peer assessment. The ratio of those submissions that the teaching assistant had to recheck was approximately 15 % in 2017. The submission that needed a recheck either didn't have all the peer assessments and self-assessments or were deemed to be rechecked because the given points differed too much. The corresponding course (Probability calculus I) in 2018 had more students and there were approximately 317 submissions per week on the average. In 2018 the ratio of those submissions that the teaching assistant had to recheck dropped below 10 %, while the activity of doing the self- and peer assessments stayed at approximately 90 %.

Time devoted to the rechecking process has been considerably diminished by implementing scripts written in Clojure and compiled to JavaScript with ClojureScript (https://clojurescript.org) to modify the behavior of the Moodle platform. This important innovation revealed time-reducing enhancements that reduced the time that manually might take an hour down to few minutes. These scripts visualize the cases that need inspection and re-evaluation by highlighting them with color-codes. This way the teaching assistants can instantly see those submissions that need manual inspection. In addition, since the scoring system of the DIGest method differs from the Moodle's default of giving the average for the three given points, this was improved by writing scripts for improving the management of calculating and forwarding the final score to the Moodle gradebook.

These scripts were written in Clojure programming language and they were compiled with ClojureScript to JavaScript programs that modify the behaviour of the Moodle. Technically this is not necessary, since all the work could still be done manually in Moodle, but the scripts greatly enhance and speed up the operations that a teaching assistant would otherwise need to do very slowly by clicking buttons and links, typing text manually and copy pasting text. As an example, using these scripts, the assistant gets in the browser window all those submissions highlighted that need to be rechecked. This way the assistant can with a single glance find all the submission that needs to be rechecked, instead of manually browsing through all of them one by one, simultaneously making the decision whether the submission should be re-evaluated. In comparison, the manual way would be very time-consuming and error-prone.

Another innovation was discovered during the process. The DIGest method doesn't use the average of the scores as the final score for the submission. However, the Moodle platform computes the average by default. This means that computing and forwarding the actual submission score to Moodle gradebook manually could take a lot of time and effort, but with the scripts the same can be done in couple of minutes. Without using the scripts, one would in practice be forced to use the default final score.

Because of the nature of statistics and mathematics, the final numerical answer is not the most important aspect of solution. Instead the most important aspect of the solution is the description how to get there, i.e. the presented path to the solution. A proposed solution can be worth of 2 points, even if the final numerical answer is not correct. This makes the model solutions constructions more challenging. Fortunately, the students seem to understand this, and questions (and answers from teaching assistants) during the peer and self-assessment stage usually clarify the complications that the nature of statistics and mathematics bring.

4. How the initiative was received

The DIGest method offers effective reflection: every student explores his/her own solutions, two other students' solutions and the model solutions. This means that a student sees several different correct and incorrect solutions which implies more and deeper learning. Student feedback of the DIGest method has been very positive. Based on feedback, 80-85% of students love the DIGest method, the rest not unequivocally, and there are also students (say 1-2%) that really hate the DIGest method.

Due to the DIGest method the number of students who interrupt courses has decreased and the number of course completions has increased. DIGest is a collaborative learning environment where every student feels to belong to the course community. In addition to peer and self-assessment, the students practice many important everyday skills like giving and receiving both positive and negative feedback. The DIGest method fits perfectly to the ideology of distance education and its e-learning implementation.

5. The learning outcomes

As an example, we consider the course Probability calculus I which is a compulsory 5 credit points course for both mathematics and statistics major students. Many students from other disciplines also take the course, and for some of them the course is compulsory. The course contents include classical probability, axioms of probability, combinatorics, conditional probability and independence, discrete and continuous random variables, expectation and variance, correlation, law of large numbers and central limit theorem. The learning objectives are to know the basics of probability (i.e. the course contents) and the most important distributions such as binomial and normal distribution. A student should be able to apply the probability concepts in different everyday problems which include random phenomena.

By using the DIGest method, the learning objectives of Probability calculus I have been achieved by solving the most of the DIGest problems and by making all required peer and self-assessments during the course. This kind of excellent course activity has implied the course grade 1/5 which is the lowest accepted grade. To earn a better grade 2-5/5, the students have taken a course exam and this way they have shown deeper understanding of the course topics. Our findings indicate that a substantial part of the students has earned grades 4-5/5 and the learning outcomes have been excellent.

We have achieved encouraging learning outcomes by using the DIGest method in the bachelor level mathematics and statistics university studies. Student feedback of the DIGest method has been very positive. The number of drop-outs, i.e. those students who interrupt courses, has decreased and the number of course completions has increased. We have clear evidence that the understanding of mathematics and statistics is better than before when using traditional exercise methods.

6. Plans to further develop the initiative

We will produce short video clips introducing the main concepts of the DIGest courses in the bachelor level mathematics and statistics. Video clips will be published in Vimeo and they will be linked to the course web pages, so that all the learning material is easily accessible. This allows the students to follow the courses at home; not even following the lectures necessities the travelling to the science campus.

So far only a few of the bachelor level mathematics courses use the DIGest method in their course exercises. Our plan is to extend the use of the DIGest method in mathematics and turn it to the main teaching method in the mathematics studies in the same way as it already is in the statistics bachelor studies.

R-programming is a central tool in the bachelor level statistics courses. For the present, R-exercises of the DIGest courses are peer and self-assessed like other exercises. In the future, this part will be improved. A considerable amount of R-exercises can be assessed automatically. In cooperation with the Computer science department the Test My Code (TMC) system can be combined to R-exercises so that the students solve problems step by step towards correct solutions. Moreover, TMC system provides automatic feedback.

References

Varvio, S.-L., Koskenoja M. and Piiroinen P. 2018. DIGest – Bachelor studies of mathematics and statistics (in Finnish). https://wiki.helsinki.fi/display/mathstatOpiskelu/DIGest, University of Helsinki.

Vihavainen A., Luukkainen M., Pärtel M. (2013) Test My Code: An Automatic Assessment Service for the Extreme Apprenticeship Method. In: Vittorini P., Gennari R., Marenzi I., Mascio T., Prieta F. (eds) 2nd International Workshop on Evidence-based Technology Enhanced Learning. Advances in Intelligent Systems and Computing, vol 218. Springer, Heidelberg

R Core Team (2017). R: A language and environment for statistical computing. R Foundation for Statistical Computing, Vienna, Austria, URL https://www.R-project.org/

Mika Koskenoja (left first), **Petteri Piiroinen** (second) and **Sirkka-Liisa Varvio** are university lecturers and **Toni Lehtonen, Aku Leivonen** (third), **Joonas Nuutinen** and **Nea Rantanen** (fourth) are students at the Department of Mathematics and Statistics of the University of Helsinki. Koskenoja and Piiroinen have PhD in mathematics and Varvio has PhD in statistics.

Presentation inControl (iControl)

Lew Sook Ling, Ooi Shih Yin, Yuwaraja Muthukumar, Md Asifur Rahman, Chew Yee Jian and Nicholas Lee Ming Ze
Multimedia University, Melaka, Malaysia
sllew@mmu.edu.my

Abstract:
Quality teachers are ones who have positive effects on student studying progress via blended teaching and learning of content, pedagogic, communications and interpersonal skills. They have integrated information technology (IT) tools in teaching and learning inside and outside the classroom. Teaching and learning while controlling IT tools such as computer, PowerPoint, Media Player, wireless presenter and etc. can be very troublesome especially when multiple tasks are in progress. The teacher usually has difficulties to juggle between controlling the computer and interacting to the students who are sitting far away from him or her. With the aim of improving interactivity between teacher and students in an integrated learning environments, this project is to design and develop a mobile app (iControl) that can remotely control a specific connected server computer for presentation. iControl aims to turn a smartphone into a presentation tool. iControl can remotely control a connected computer for presentation on the go. Among the usages of the app include functioning as a controller for mouse, keyboard, presentation, media player, camera for current screenshot, file transfer, file downloader and system power. In order to connect the server, both personal computer or laptop and Android phone must be connected on the same network through Wi-Fi. When Wi-Fi network is unavailable, user can use Android hotspot in order to connect to personal computer or laptop. An empirical test of 196 students has been carried out for investigating the effectiveness of the developed mobile app. The results show improvement on interactivity between teacher and students with the developed mobile app.

1. Introduction

1.1 Overview

Presentations are conducted using the conventional input devices such as mouse, keyboards, laser pointer or advanced devices such as wireless mouse, wireless keyboard and Wi-Fi presenter. Smartphones are economically famous among all over the population in the world. This is because of the features such as camera, Wi-Fi, games, Bluetooth, Video recorder and etc. (Barde et al., 2014).

Bring Your Own Device (BYOD) system has been around for a while and is gaining momentum as more and more businesses opt for the system. Under the BYOD structure, the first thing that comes to mind is cost savings in different forms. In most cases, a mobile device can be turned into a gadget for business use. If that is the case, the business saves on buying the devices.

This project, Presentation inControl (iControl) turns a tablet or smartphone into a presentation tool. iControl can remotely control a connected computer for presentation on the go. Among the usages of the apps include functioning as a controller for mouse, keyboard, presentation, media player, camera for current screenshot, file transfer, file downloader and system power.

1.2 Project Objectives
The main objective of this project is to develop a mobile app that can remotely control a specific connected server computer for improving interactivity during presentation. The features are stated below:

- Mouse, keyboard, media player and system power controller
- Touch/drag as laser pointer
- Pinch to zoom
- Shake to proceed to next slide
- Camera for screenshot
- Send files from computer to Android and vice versa
- Multi User mode only available for (Keyboard, power point control, Media control
- Power saving mode for reducing power consumption

2. The Infrastructure

2.1 Software Development Methodology
System Development Life Cycle (SDLC) is the selected methodology. SDLC is a much detailed process taking charge of important projects where the process of documentation, training, principles and security are practiced and adopted by this project (ptiWebTech, 2015; Young, 2013).

2.2 Programming Languages
Java can create advanced and independent applications for both desktop and android applications (Chaurasia, 2016). Java also involves in creating network connection applications by using socket programming, HTTP, FTP and etc. (NetBeans, 2015). Hence, Java will be suitable and better for both Android and Desktop application.

2.3 Database
Server application has a function to save and store the user connection passwords and download file paths. In order to save this data, notepad is used as a database module. The data will be stored as a text file in internal storage of the user's personal computer.

2.4 Flowchart Diagram
Figure 1 shows the flowchart of the Android application (Client-side).

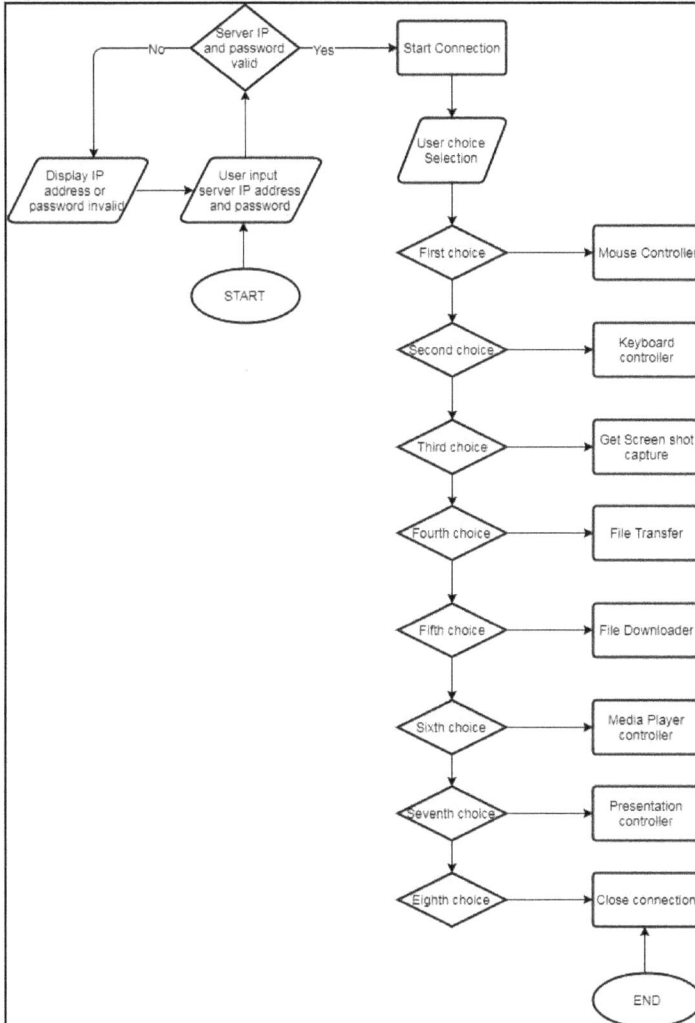

Figure 1: Flowchart for Client-side (Android) Application Menu

Figure 2 shows the flowchart of the PC application (Server-side).

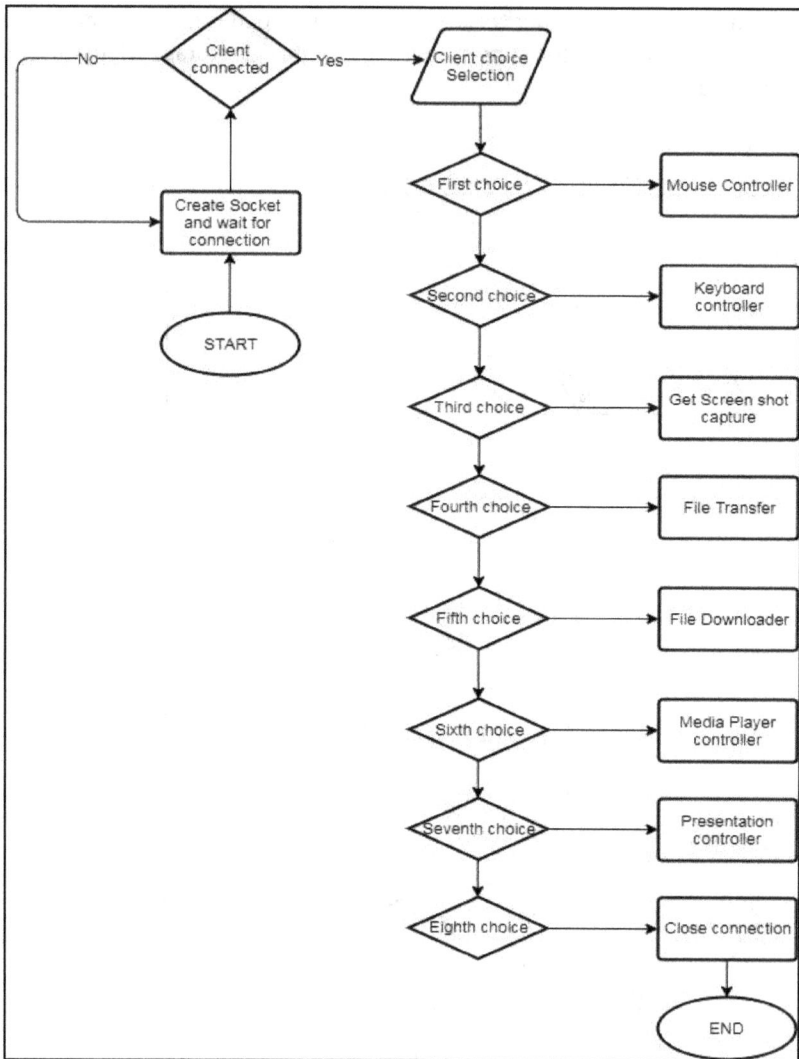

Figure 2: Flowchart for Server-side (PC or Laptop) Control Menu

2.5 Requirements for Application Development

Software Requirement
Android Studio was used to create the Android application. Features such as graphical layout editing, NDK support, keystore management and APK signing in were activated by this software (Singh, Sharma, & Singh, 2016).
NetBeans IDE was used to develop PC application. NetBeans GUI builder and NetBeans platform were used as they are the most efficient combination to build up a better desktop Swing application (NetBeans, 2015).

Hardware Requirements

Android application: An android smartphone with a minimum of 1.0 GHz CPU speed, 1 GB RAM and 512 MB of free space of internal memory.

PC application: A personal computer with a minimum of 2.3 GHz CPU speed, 2 GB RAM and 0 GB of free space of hard disk.

2.6 Overall Framework

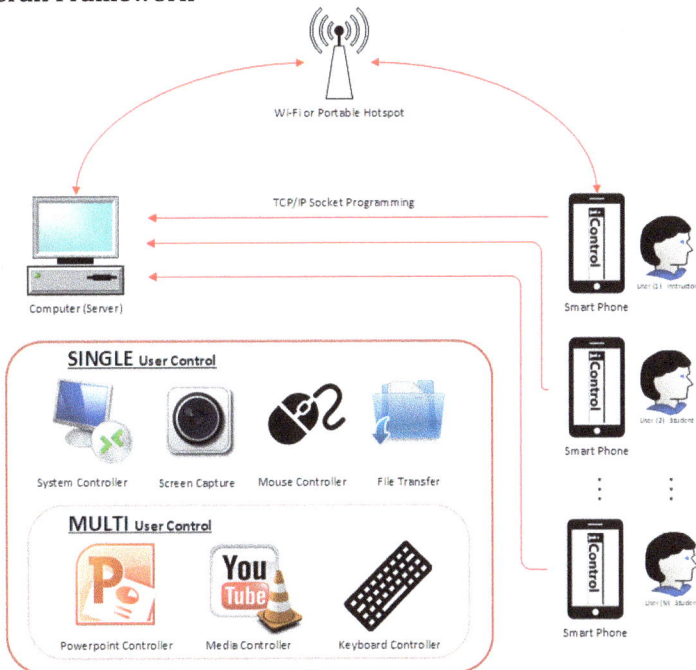

Figure 3: Overall iControl Diagram

3. The Challenges

3.1 Major Issue

In spite of many research (Pedersen, et al., 2016; Yu, et al., 2016; Ravé, et al., 2016; Roussou & Slater, 2017) have been conducted to identify the factors of improving interactivity using IT tools, but the delivery methods and use of the IT tools are generally antiquated and ineffective particularly in solving the issues of student-teacher interaction (Lee, et al., 2015).

Hence, creating a conducive T and L environment does not just depend on implementing technology in a traditional classroom, rather it depends mostly on the mechanism that learning technology is being delivered to students. Hence, technology should create a driving force in changing the interaction among the teacher and students that were lacking in the traditional T and L environment.

3.2 Teaching and Learning Issues

Teaching of lecture slides from the teacher to student and presentation of project or assignment to students or audiences while controlling the computer or laptop is troublesome especially multiple tasks are in progress. Teacher or presenter is always standing beside the computer or laptop for controlling the computer or laptop during presentation. The distance between the presenter or teacher and students is far and this distance becomes a barrier for teaching and learning interactivity.

Using devices such as mouse, keyboard, USB cables, laser pointer and presenter for presentation become an additional cost for business. More devices used will have higher possibility of hardware damages and maintenance costs. As compared to one own device or BYOD structure used in this project, money is saved when hardware and maintenance costs are transferred to employees when they use their own devices.

3.3 Existing Applications as Competitors

Similar applications were compared between different remote control applications (including iControl) (Asus, 2016; BeApps Mobile, 2017; Chaurasia, 2016; Google Play, 2017; Remote Control Open Source, 2017; TeamViewer, 2005; Urs, 2016). As shown in Table 3.1, all the apps were developed in an android platform. As an analysis, majority of the apps are using Wi-Fi as a communication medium in order to remotely control the PC. As an advantage of using Wi-Fi, it secures the data of the device. There are more application features as a media and power point controllers. These features are necessary and needed by majority of users. As a least feature stated by the Table 3.1, receiving current snapshot from the PC are not developed by the existing applications. This feature is the most important to get a quick look of the PC's current state. Popular presentation tools were also compared between the presentation tools (including iControl). As displayed in Table 3.2, only iControl is suitable for classroom setting and can improve interaction between presenter and audiences.

Table 1: Comparison of Remote Control Application

	Mouse	Keyboard	Snapshot	File Transfer	System Power Controller	Media Controller	Power Point Controller	Last Updated	Installed
Team Viewer	✓	✓		✓		✓	✓	2018	10,000,000
VLC Mobile Remote	✓			✓		✓		2018	1,000,000
ASUS Remote Link	✓	✓				✓	✓	2017	10,000,000
DMKHO Remote Control	✓					✓		2017	100
Remote Control[Open Source]	✓				✓	✓		2014	100
MPC-HC Remote	✓			✓		✓	✓	2012	100,000
PPT Remote	✓						✓	2017	50,000
Wi-Fi Presentation Remote							✓	2018	50,000
iControl	✓	✓	✓	✓	✓	✓	✓	2018	

Table 2: Comparison of Presentation Tools versus Remote Control Application

	Remote Desktop	Mobile Application Presenter	Normal Wireless Presenter
Example	Team Viewer	iControl	Logitech Wireless Presenter
Connection	Internet / Local	Intranet (Wi-Fi / Hotspot)	USB (Bluetooth)
Connection Stability	DEPENDS on Internet / Data Connectivity	STABLE	STABLE
Purpose	Connect to a PC which are in ANOTHER LOCATION	Simple Control of PC + Wireless Power Point Control	Wireless Power Point Control (Additional features with extra $)
Suitability in Classroom	X	✓	✓
Product Price	FREE	FREE / (RM 0.99 / 1 time)	$ 20~$ 100+ Approx. (RM 50 ~ RM 400+)

4. Testing Of Participants on Icontrol

The Cronbach's Alpha measures with all above 0.70, indicating internal consistency reliabilities (Bowling, 2009; Sekaran, 2003). Completed surveys were received from 190 individuals (96.9%). After treating the missing data using list wise deletion; leaving 188 questionnaires (95.9%) for analysis.

Based on the questionnaire, from a total score of 5.0, all the mean scores were increased (Attitude: 3.2 to 4.5 points, Interest: 3.1 to 4.6, Knowledge: 3.5 to 4.7).

In order to test the effectiveness of iControl, a written test which consists of 5 structured questions of a university subject was conducted for the respondents of "with" and "without" iControl. From a mean score of a total of 10 marks, "with" group scored a mean score of 8.5 while the "without" group scored only 6.6.

5. The Learning Outcomes

5.1 Completed Solutions
Table 3 explains the completed working prototypes of iControl.

Table 3: Main Features of iControl

Feature	Screenshot	Description
System Processes		This represents the login process in android application by getting the server IP address and port number from users. If the user's input is not a valid IP address or port number, the system will prompt an error message to instruct the user. The system will also prompt an unreachable warning message if the server's IP is unreachable. The IP searching process depends on device's IP identification time. The process will finish in seconds if the IP is in reachable distance.
Menu Page		This menu page allows easy access to any one of the main features.

Feature	Screenshot	Description
PowerPoint Controller		The communication processes in all the features are done by delivering commands to the server computer when user presses the buttons on their mobile phone. This is the remote control for PowerPoint presentation activity. Presenter features such as "Back", "Play", "Forward", "Pointer", "Escape" are available. "Shake" the phone is also enabled for fast command to move to the next slide.
Media Controller		This represents media control activity. Three common players are available: YouTube VLC Player Media Classic Player

Feature	Screenshot	Description
	Media Controller / Youtube / VLC Player / Media Classic Player	
Keyboard		This represents keyboard activity. Keyboard process is done by sending the keycode commands to server computer by user. The green coloured button indicates the long press by user to execute hold button process in PC keyboard.
Typing in Keyboard		This is the third page of keyboard. This process is not the same as the keyboard button typing as above feature. This activity uses Android API keyboard in order to type the characters. This will enable users to type emoji as displayed in the screenshot.

Lew Sook Ling et al.

Feature	Screenshot	Description
Mouse		This represents mouse control activity. Users can use their fingers to touch and drag in mouse pad area. The mouse pad area will capture the x, y positions when user touches. The client will send the command codes to the server computer immediately. The codes will be executed in the server side using robot and move the mouse remotely. The codes sending progress will be ended when user lifts up their fingers from the mousepad. If the users use double touch to scroll or fling, the program will send the y position send the codes to server. When the server receives y positions, it will execute scrolling function remotely. The green button indicates a long pressed by user to executed hold click in the server side.
Screenshot Capture		This represents screenshot capture activity. When user presses the snap icon, current screenshot is captured. The image can be dragged, moved and zoomed by user.

142

Feature	Screenshot	Description
File Transfer		This represents file picking process in file transferring activity. User can pick the file from the Android file browser and send to server computer.
File Downloader		This represents file downloading process. User can download file from the

Feature	Screenshot	Description
		server computer to Android phone. The file will be stored in "iControl" folder.
System Power		This represents system power control to sever computer from Android application [client]. This activity consists of 4 power options such as "sleep" mode, "power off", "lock/log off" mode and "restart" mode. By clicking any of these button and after getting confirmation by the user, the command will be executed by the server system immediately.

Feature	Screenshot	Description
Power Saving Mode - Grey Scale		Power saving mode is available. This mode can reduce about 41% of power consumption. This mode works on AMOLED screen. The black pixels are the LEDs that are turned off (Triggsoctober, 2014).
Multi User Mode		Multi User mode is also available for Keyboard, PowerPoint and Media control. More than 1 up to 255 users are allowed to control concurrently.

5.2 Overall Learning Outcomes

Presentation inControl (iControl) is a project that enables BYOD structure to business. By using this mobile app, users are able to remotely control their machines wherever and whenever as they are connected to the same Wi-Fi network on both devices for presentation. The main objectives of this project is to provide an innovative application that can improve interactivity between presenter and audiences and reduce costs for devices and maintenance of presentation tools.

As a long way in this research, a lot of information gathering were done by collecting some of the existing applications for Android. This application was tested by connection, sensitivity, features and interfaces. By conducting this research, some of the important information gathered such as advantages, disadvantages, features comparison between iControl and existing applications. This information gathering enhances this project by understanding user's needs.

Moreover, this application was developed by using System Development Life Cycle (SDLC) methodology. This methodology were helpful to complete this project by using this SDLC phases and the steps provided. A lot of requirement were listed in order to develop this project. An improvised methods and information gathering were learned to develop this project in a professional manner.

Furthermore, this application was well planned and designed in a professional way with the help of three UML diagrams. Activity, Flowchart and Context diagrams are the system designs of this project. This diagrams are the summarize part of this project and well explain the application's system architecture. A lot of knowledge gained by implementing this diagrams.

This is a TCP server client architecture applied project by communicating between two devices using socket programming. Android works as the client-side as a remote controller for users and PC works as the server-side to receive commands from client-side. This commands are interpreted and executed by this server-side to accomplish user's controls.

As a conclusion, this application will reduce the use of some of the external wired devices. This application will be very helpful for many kinds of users such as employees from different fields, students and lecturers. It is hoped that this application will be able to be more effective to achieve the objectives in a positive manner.

6. Recommendations

Human-Human interaction was improved by engaging students with their teachers via iControl without investigating on Human-System perspective. Hence, future study is recommended to incorporate features enhancing Human-System interaction provided in an integrated learning environment.

References

Asus. (2016). How to connect the ZenFone and your laptop via Remote Link? | Official Support | ASUS Global. Retrieved August 22, 2017, from https://www.asus.com/support/FAQ/1007490/

Barde, L., Dhole, N., Waghmare, P., & Suryawanshi, S. (2014). Controlling PC/Laptop via Android Phone (Android Remote Control), 3(1), 2806–2809.

BeApps Mobile. (2017). BeApps Mobile - Home | Facebook. Retrieved August 22, 2017, from https://www.facebook.com/beappsmobile/

Bowling, A. (2009). Research Methods in Health: Investigating Health and Health Services. 3rd ed. Berkshire: Open University Press.

Chaurasia, S. (2016). Implementation of Remote Desktop Utility using Teamviewer, 25–28. DMKHO. (2013). DMKHO software. Retrieved August 22, 2017, from http://dmkho.tripod.com/ Hlousek, M. (2014). Martin Hloušek :: Home page. Retrieved August 22, 2017, from http://hlousek.org/ Karandikar, K. (1995). Java in Education. EDC385G Interactive Multimedia Design & Production.

Google Play. (2017, August 6). Retrieved from https://play.google.com/store/search?q=remote%20control&hl=en

Lee, W. H., Kuo, M. C. & Hsu, C. C. (2015). An In-Classroom Interactive Learning Platform by Near Field Communication. Colombo, s.n., pp. 360-364.

NetBeans. (2015). NetBeans IDE. Features, (Jsr 299), 1–3. Retrieved from https://netbeans.org/features/java/

Pedersen, M. K. et al. (2016). DiffGame : Game-based Mathematics Learning for Physics. València, Spain, s.n.

ptiWebTech. (2015). Essential aspects of SDLC with its phases and models. - PTI WebTech. Retrieved August 27, 2017, from https://www.ptiwebtech.com/blog/essential-aspects-of-sdlc-with-its-phases-and-models/

Ravé, E. d., Jiménez-Hornero, F., Ariza-Villaverde, A. & Taguas-Ruiz, J. (2016). DiedricAR: A Mobile Augmented Reality System Designed for the Ubiquitous Descriptive Geometry Learning. Multimedia Tools and Applications, 75(16), pp. 9641-9663.

Remote Control Open Source. (2017). Remote Control PC[Open Source] – Android Apps on Google Play. Retrieved August 22, 2017, from https://play.google.com/store/apps/details?id=de.pro_open.remotecontrol

Roussou, M. & Slater, M. (2017). Comparison of the Effect of Interactive versus Passive Virtual Reality Learning Activities in Evoking and Sustaining Conceptual Change. s.l., IEEE Computer Society, pp. 1-11.

Sekaran, U. (2003). Research Methods for Business: A Skill Building Approach. 4th ed. s.l.:John Wiley and Sons.

Singh, A., Sharma, S., & Singh, S. (2016). Android Application Development using Android Studio and PHP Framework. International Journal of Computer Applications Recent Trends in Future Prospective in Engineering & Management Technology, 975–8887.

TeamViewer. (2005). TeamViewer – Remote Support, Remote Access, Service Desk, Online Collaboration and Meetings. Retrieved August 22, 2017, from https://www.teamviewer.com/en/

Triggsoctober, R., 2014. Android Authority. [Online] Available at: https://www.androidauthority.com/black-amoled-display-power-saving-541984/ [Accessed 26 September 2018].

Lew Sook Ling et al.

Urs, A. (2016). VLC Mobile Remote - PC & Mac for Android - Free download and software reviews - CNET Download.com. Retrieved August 6, 2017, from http://download.cnet.com/VLC- Mobile-Remote-PC-Mac/3000-2094_4-76643142.html

Young, D. (2013). Software Development Methodologies, 1–10.

Yu, C. H., Liao, Y. T. & Wu, C. C. (2016). Using Augmented Reality to Learn the Enumeration Strategies of Cubes. Bangkok, s.n., pp. 412-418.

Author Biography

Dr. Lew Sook Ling is working as senior lecturer in Multimedia University, Malaysia. She has authored, co-authored and reviewed several national and international publications. She has received several international awards such as ITEX17, ITEX18, PECIPTA15 and PECIPTA17. Her research interest involves educational technology, business intelligence, information science and technology.

Joining the Dots: Where e-Portfolios meet Programmatic Assessment

Panos Vlachopoulos
Macquarie University, Sydney, Australia
panos.vlachopoulos@mq.edu.au

Abstract

Universities Australia but also globally are looking into designing, developing and implementing sustainable and pedagogically meaningful approaches to holistic or programmatic assessment in their curricula. The use of an electronic portfolio (e-portfolio) tool, the provision of longitudinal tutorial support, and credible feedback are often the key design challenges for programmatic assessment. At Macquarie University, the Faculty of Medicine and Health Sciences designed, developed, and implemented a pedagogically sound and technologically workable and sustainable solution to programmatic (holistic) assessment using an e-portfolio tool for its newly established Bachelor of Clinical Science. This case study presents the objectives, challenges, and key lessons learned from the 2 year implementation of an e-portfolio tool to assess capabilities and promote reflective practice in a cohort of undergraduate students.

1. Introduction

Medical Schools across the country but also globally are looking into designing, developing, and implementing a programmatic assessment approach (Var De Vleuten et al, 2012) to their medical curricula. This approach is often part of a continuum, which begins with the development of specific capabilities for graduates, necessary to get accredited as a Doctor or Health Care practitioner, and then align this with learning activities and measurable assessment opportunities across a program of study. The use of an electronic portfolio tool, the provision of longitudinal tutorial support and credible feedback are often the key design challenges for programmatic assessment (Bok et al, 2013). The objective of the initiative described in this case study was to design, develop, implement and evaluate a pedagogically sound and technologically workable and sustainable solution to programmatic assessment using an electronic portfolio tool across an entire Faculty in an Australian University. The process involved several stages: a systematic review of the literature around programmatic assessment and the use of electronic portfolios, a needs analysis process and evaluation of the functionality of several e-portfolio tools, a team-based approach to designing materials and learning and assessment resources as well as delivering training; and a strategic plan for diffusion of the innovation across the university, other universities and e-portfolio providers.

2. What is the context and scale of this initiative?

The Faculty of Medicine and Health Sciences is a newly formed Faculty at Macquarie University. As part of the Faculty's expansion of educational offerings, a number of programs have been developed or are currently under development: including an innovative undergraduate Bachelor Program in Clinical Sciences, a Master of Public Health, and an innovative Doctor of Medicine (MD). The learning innovation team worked under the direction of the Associate Dean Learning and Teaching, the Faculty's Executive Dean and Program Directors to provide a Faculty-Wide technological solution to Programmatic Assessment which is aligned with the University's Learning and Teaching Strategy but also with contemporary thinking in Medical Education. The project reported here commenced in support for a workable and innovative solution to the need for programmatic Assessment initially for the Bachelor of Clinical Science Program. It gradually expanded to impact on the development of the other two postgraduate programs across the Faculty. During the process the innovative idea was diffused across Macquarie University Hospital as part of its Continuum Professional Development process for its nurses and the need to record their activities systematically in an e-portfolio tool. It is now part of a greater project across all Faculties at Macquarie University but also across three more Medical Schools in Australia with direct consultation with e-portfolio service providers.

3. The infrastructure

Macquarie University commenced its attempt to introduce a program-wide approach to learning, teaching and assessment with the use of an electronic portfolio more than 5 years ago (McNeill & Cram, 2011). Whereas at the time key stakeholders, including students and academics, saw value in such an approach to learning, major technological barriers at the time as well as a culture of silos in the way innovative ideas were promoted and often executed made further implementation impossible. Our approach was different. Armed with an innovative and ambitious Learning and Teaching Strategy that advocates a program-based design and a 'connected curriculum' and 'connected people' ethos we strategically developed an approach to staff and student capability development that included:

- Early buy in and full engagement of the Faculty's Executive Dean, Associate Dean Learning and Teaching, and the Faculty Manager. This was an important first step to ensure that the new academic staff were on board and included as part of this innovation.

- Establishment of a steering committee for the curriculum development of the programs in question, which oversees the design, development and implementation of the e-portfolio. This committee included academics, learning designers, and student support services.
- Closed collaboration with various e-portfolio vendors, the University's IT team and the Learning Innovation Hub to decide on the platform that best suits our needs.
- Development of resources, including manuals and templates, which are open to all Faculties to re-purpose and re-use. This was essential to avoid duplication of effort.
- Implementation of training sessions for Faculty's Tutors, and ongoing training for students, through a train the trainer approach (the trained Faculty tutors became the trainers of the students, future students will become tutors to new students)
- Open and ongoing communication and collaboration with the central University's IT team and the University's Learning Innovation Hub.
- Open and ongoing communication and collaboration with the chosen e-portfolio provider, which involved various visits and training events not only for the Faculty of Medicine but also the rest of the Faculties and central support teams.
- Development of a community of practice in e-portfolio within Macquarie University, which resulted in a joint Strategic Learning Innovation Grant. This is an active community that provides the forum for showcases and sharing of good practice.

Good progress was made in terms of changing the culture towards implementation of e-portfolios through honest and open collaboration and a clear strategic pedagogical need. The fact that many programs across the Faculty of Medicine and Health Sciences and other Faculties across the University are now looking to implement an e-portfolio approach to learning and assessment plus the university wide and national impact are illustrative of this change.

4. The Challenges

There were three key challenges, which we faced as part of the implementation and further expansion of the initiative reported here. The challenges and the way we worked to overcome them are presented below.

1. Interoperability and Integration

Interoperability is the ability for two systems to understand each other and to use the functionality of each other. In our case, we were interested in having the following types of integration:

- Single Sign On from the Learning Management System (also referred to as Virtual Learning Environment to the student e-portfolio interface.
- Single Sign On from the Learning Management System to the tutor e-portfolio interface (for assessment purposes)
- Creation of e-portfolio accounts upon single sign on for new users
- The automatic and periodic export of new students work from the Learning Management system to their e-portfolio.
- The ability to create e-portfolio artefacts from content and activities directly transferred from the Learning Management system (e.g. reflection on a quiz or an online discussion forum)

Our chosen e-portfolio provider supported a number of the required integrations needed to enable a pedagogically meaningful approach to programmatic assessment. However, our license agreement did not allow for full integration of the Learning Management System with the e-portfolio. This was a decision made for both financial and technical reasons beyond the power of the learning design team to influence. In practice what we had was a smooth single sign on for both students and tutors from the LMS to the e-portfolio and the ability to bulk enrol users from one system to the other. There was no integration as far as content and activities were concerned and no ability to transfer grades and other student data from one system to the other. We worked out a 'framework' to motivate students to periodically export their work from the LMS into their e-portfolio in order to reflect and receive feedback from tutors and professional mentors. The framework included:

- A list of capability statements and expectations for student to be evidenced at given deadline during their program of study. For example, we asked our students to bring evidence from their work in their program about how they develop their approach to citizenship (see Figure 1) by specifically reflecting on key aspects of digital technology.
- A set of purposefully designed templates within the e-portfolio tool, which were set to be auto-submitted at the submission deadline (See Figure 2). The template required students to bring the relevant evidence from their work (e.g. a marked piece of assessment, an activity that they

completed), and then engage with a number of prompt reflective questions.

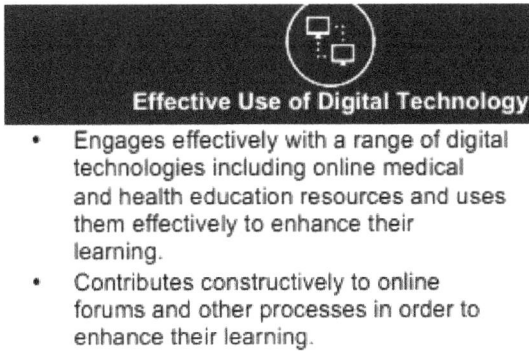

Effective Use of Digital Technology

- Engages effectively with a range of digital technologies including online medical and health education resources and uses them effectively to enhance their learning.
- Contributes constructively to online forums and other processes in order to enhance their learning.

Figure 1: Sample Capability Statements as they appear on the e-portfolio tool

Following the framework and using the bespoke templates, students had to transfer all relevant work from their Learning Management System to their e-portfolio, reflect, and develop action plans for continuous improvement. The limitation of not having the ability to transfer the work from one system to another automatically resulted in some technical issues (e.g. how to transfer quiz results or questions, how to transfer marked assignments from our text matching software TurnitIn). The only possible solution was a low tech approach using screenshots and downloading and re-uploading pdf versions of student submissions.

Scholar

Expectation at mid year 1
- Describes the function of research and the role of evidence in knowledge creation
- Engages with and completes the individual and group set tasks in the professional practice unit
- Engages competently with the e-portfolio assessment system

When searching for and reporting on information:
- Formulates and applies appropriate information searching strategies in relevant medical and research databases
- Uses appropriate citation standards

---

mQ Assessed Evidence

Fill in each cell below every time you add an asset/evidence. The cells are narrow, the key is to be succinct. Remember all your evidence needs to be clearly and directly related to the identified aspect. Both accomplishments and areas of growth have been unpacked. You also need to develop an action plan to address feedback and/or your development in this aspect/capability.

mQ Assessed evidence title + description + date you added evidence to this table. e.g. MEDI204 AT2 Case Study Report 25/09/16	How does your evidence relate to this aspect?	Identify growth - areas of improvement or strength	Develop an action plan to address feedback and/or your development in this aspect/capability
MEDI103 AT1 communication analysis 06/07/17	This also relates to the 2nd dot point of the scholar capability as this is a completed individual assessment that was compulsory for each student enrolled in the unit to complete to go towards the final mark. Thus, completing this assessment shows my engagement in the professional practice unit by participating in set individual task that the unit specifically provides.	Growth areas that require improvement would definitely be my grammar and punctuation as well as practice planning major pints before writing an essay or writing task to ultimately benefit the thinking process of what to write to specifically make sense.	1. Plan and Practice more essays under strict conditions 2. Re-read when finished to make sure it makes sense and appropriate to the question 3. Edit and eliminate any mistakes or unnecessary information that may affect the overall mark or perspective of the essay such as making it more construed and unclear.

Figure 2: Sample template as it was submitted in the e-portfolio tool by a student.

2. Sustainability

To develop our sustainability model for the programmatic assessment and e-portfolio innovation we drew upon the "three pillars" of sustainable development (Adams, 2006; Robertson, 2008, p. 819): resource management, educational attainment and professional development. We presented our business case to the Executive Team in the Faculty of Medicine and Health Sciences.:

- Resource management: We created a Faculty Resource Centre on the e-Portfolio tool, which allowed for different members of academic and professional staff to view and edit resources. We made sure that our resources were designed in a way and format that would allow:

redeployment (using the same content without the need to change them at all in similar contexts; e.g. we used the same guidelines across all units in the Bachelor of Clinical Science), re-arrangement (we arranged and slightly modified content to allow use in new contexts; e.g. we made some changes to the guides to be used in the postgraduate offerings) and repurposing (we took the same content and used it in new ways; e.g used the guides as resources for discussions with other Medical Schools across the country).

- Professional Development: we offered a comprehensive faculty development and support program and a set of strategies that include developing shared understanding of philosophies and technological affordances; encouraging active practice; continuous reflection; and development of shared vocabularies. We were confident that a critical mass that understands and uses e-portfolios would be able to support us in the case of staff mobility.

- Educational Attainment: we placed a strong emphasis on sustained educational benefits. We linked the implementation of programmatic assessment and e-portfolios with clear career pathways and our capability frameworks. As the student voices in the video illustrate, the use of the e-portfolio was associated strongly with professional growth. We also included student evaluations, including frequent feedback sessions throughout the sessions as well as end of semester evaluations.

We were clear from the outset that the introduction of programmatic assessment and the use of electronic portfolios will grow in demand and we plan our approach to meet this demand. We predicted a growth in number from 40 to 400 students over a period of 3 years and secured the funds for this from central and Faculty budgets.

3. Reproducibility
Two examples are directly relevant as to how our initiative can be re-produced. The first is related to a whole of a University approach, the second is related to a Medicine and Health as a discipline

- Whole of university approach: As part of the development of a greater community of practice interested in implementing electronic portfolios for sound pedagogical reasons, a team of learning designers and academics from across the Faculties at Macquarie University were awarded a Strategic Priority Grant under the title: Digital Health: connecting disciplines with the workplace and leading digital innovation in clinical education programs. This was one of three e-portfolio and programmatic design or assessment related projects. (see Appendix A). The project aims to bring together all clinical assessment components across the university and further explore the potential of e-portfolios as a credible and reliable tool for programmatic assessment, building on the work done in the Faculty of Medicine and Health Sciences.

- Whole of discipline approach: we built a strong collaboration with three additional Australian Universities to explore how electronic portfolios can support programmatic assessment in ways which will allow more valid and reliable assessment offline, using mobile apps in clinical settings. The working group has been established to build upon our existing resources, templates and training materials and make them available for offline and online mobile use. We have also included other aspect for e-portfolio technical improvements which we now negotiate as a consortium of prestigious universities directly with an eportfolio provided.

Throughout the process of our initiative we learnt that transparency, open and honest discussions and networking are crucial in achieving reproducibility. We have presented our initial ideas across the various Faculties and Committees at MQ, and at national and international conferences, including the Australian eportfolios Forum and Ascilite Conference. We have listened and acted upon the feedback and comments, avoiding mistakes that others have done earlier and building on advice we received from experts in the field, both educators and technical experts.

5. Learning Outcomes and Student success

The quality of the learning experience is more important than the medium of learning. When it comes to student learning outcomes and success we were interested in finding out how does this innovation change the way in which students think about reflective practice, feedback and professional growth across an entire program as opposed to merely investigating usability of the tool and usage data in particular units of study. To this end, we implemented frequent in session evaluation activities, which involved feedback sessions with tutors, some anonymous evaluations using polling devices such as Socrative and focus groups with all students in the Bachelor of Clinical Science and their tutors.

The following anonymised quotes have been taken directly from end of program focus groups in relation to their personal and professional growth:

"The more I began to reflect, however, the more I began to understand its importance. I soon found myself reflecting on everything and not because I had to but because I wanted to. Reflection has actually now become a large part of the way I work and has allowed me to truly understand my ambitions, values and principles." (Student, BClinSc, 2017)

"While the portfolio at first seemed quite tedious, as I progressed through the session being equipped with the skills to reflect effectively I was able to draw personal meaning and the process of reflection became easier. I have come to enjoy the e-portfolio experience and would strongly encourage this resource to be continued with all cohorts." (Student, BClinSc, 2017)

"I feel like I found the portfolio pretty hard at first, and it was a little bit unnatural reflecting on pretty much every assignment I did. But I feel like the second portfolio, that's when it really clicked for me, and I saw that it was more like just evidence of the capability that I now had. And as I reflected, my marks also improved, and so I thought it was really useful. And now for the graduation portfolio, I feel like, with each capability, the more difficult they are, it becomes more meaningful with the portfolio because it shows all the best evidence that we have. That's all" (Student, BClinSc, 2017)

The end of unit evaluation data "Learner Experience of Unit' implemented by the Teaching Evaluation for Development Services (TEDs) was completed by 75% of the student cohort. The vast majority of students (80% of the students who completed the questionnaire) mentioned the experience of e-portfolio as the most useful form of feedback they received across the program of study.

We need to remind ourselves that the implementation of the e-portfolio is designed for longitudinal impact as far as feedback and reflection are concerned. To this end, the biggest evidence of success will be the impact that their portfolio had in helping them making the right future study or career choices. We also need to remind ourselves that no one "off the shelf" tool will meet all the needs for all stakeholders. What is important is to work with the chosen provider in creative ways (usually through learning design) to make best pedagogical use of the tool. The alternative option of creating bespoke systems using in-house resources is both time consuming and not a cost effective solution.

6. Plans to further develop the initiative

As far as further technical development is concerned, we are working to ensure full integration between our Learning Management System and our chosen e-portfolio tool. This will save both students and tutors enormous effort when transferring content and data from one system to the other. Further development of templates to incorporate new features of the tool (e.g. opportunity to work offline using templates for a mobile app) will be required.

In relation to human resources, we will continue to build capacity for tutors and mentors in assessing using an e-portfolio. We were also positively surprised with the digital competency of our students to the level that we want to include them as designers in the next revision of our portfolio templates and as tutors for our new cohort of students.

Acknowledgements
I would like to thank my colleague Sherrie Love, Senior Learning Designer in the Faculty of Medicine and Health Science, for her invaluable support with this project. Many thanks also to the Bachelor of Clinical Science Professional Practice Team, under the leadership of Dr Sarah White, for working with me to implement programmatic assessment and providing all the academic support to make this initiative a success.

References
Adams, W, 2006, "The future of sustainability: Re-thinking environment and development in the twenty-first century". Retrieved from the International Union for Conservation of Nature website: http://cmsdata.iucn.org/downloads/iucn_future_of_sustanability.pdf

Bok HG, Teunissen PW, Favier RP, Rietbroek NJ, Theyse LF, Brommer H, Haarhuis JC, van Beukelen P, van der Vleuten CP, Jaarsma DA, 2013, "Programmatic assessment of competency-based workplace learning: When theory meets practice." BMC Med Educ 13:123

McNeill, M. & Cram, A, 2011, "Evaluating E-portfolios for university learning: Challenges and Opportunities". In G. Williams, P. Statham, N. Brown & B. Cleland (Eds.), Changing Demands, Changing Directions. Proceedings Ascilite Hobart, pp.862-873.

Van der Vleuten CPM, Schuwirth LWT, Driessen EW, Dijkstra J, Tigelaar D, Baartman LKJ, Van Tartwijk J. 2012, "A model for programmatic assessment fit for purpose" Med Teach, vol 34, pp.205–214.

Author biography

Associate **Professor Panos Vlachopoulos** is Associate Dean, Quality and Standards Faculty of Arts at Macquarie University. Panos is an academic educator with 15 years of international experience in the area of Higher Education Development. He has led large-scale curriculum development projects in the UK, New Zealand, Hong Kong, Greece and Australia. His research interests include online learning design, online facilitation, social network analysis and professional development.

Managing HIV: From Dull To Digital

Natalie Martyn
Programme Manager, SAHCS, South Africa
natalie@sahivsoc.org

Abstract

South Africa has the biggest and most high-profile HIV epidemic in the world, with an estimated 7.1 million people living with HIV in 2016. South Africa accounts for a third of all new HIV infections in Southern Africa. In 2016, there were 270,000 new HIV infections and 110,000 South Africans died from AIDS-related illnesses.

South Africa has the largest antiretroviral treatment (ART) programme in the world and these efforts have been largely financed from its own domestic resources. In 2015, the country was investing more than $1.34 billion annually to run its HIV programmes.

Over three decades, South Africa has substantially improved access to antiretroviral therapy (ART), as well as expanded access to circumcision, condoms, PrEP and other prevention programmes, with a reduction in new infections by 44% in the recent Human Sciences Research Council (HSRC) report over the 5-year period from 2012 to 2017.

Improved ART access, the vast majority of it initiated by nurses, and the hopeful HSRC data, obscure the large group of "missing 90s" within the HIV continuum of care, especially those among men and young people, who are less likely to test and initiate treatment timeously.

The reasons for these missing groups not engaging in care is complex but include issues such as poor accessibility (including having facilities open during non-working hours) and perceived lack of quality care. While certain initiatives, such as same-day initiation of ART by nurses have gained traction, others such as PrEP (the use of antiretroviral drugs to protect HIV-negative people from infection), have had limited success.

Although UNAIDS estimates that new HIV infections in adults decreased by a modest 11% between 2010 and 2016, the Global Burden of Disease Study 2015 investigators found no meaningful decrease in new HIV infections in the previous decade. The coming demographic wave, as children become adolescents and young adults, threatens major expansions of the epidemic. In 2016, 43% of the population in low-income countries, 43% of the population in all of sub-Saharan Africa (excluding high-income countries), and 31% of the population in lower-middle income countries were younger than 15 years.

Natalie Martyn

Far from putting the world on course to vanquish AIDS, existing approaches are leaving numerous populations behind. In sub-Saharan Africa, young people and men of all ages consistently have suboptimal outcomes along the HIV treatment continuum. Various marginalised populations at increased risk of HIV infection, including gay and bisexual men, people who inject drugs, sex workers, transgender people, and the sex partners of people in these groups, accounted for 44% of new HIV infections worldwide (80% of new infections outside sub-Saharan Africa).

Contrary to optimistic expectations of ending AIDS, these trends point toward the likelihood of a much more concerning scenario. Although the desired benefits of population-level viral suppression could be realised in settings and populations where access to HIV testing and treatment services is widespread, those people living in countries or belonging to marginalised populations in which services are difficult or impossible to obtain will remain highly vulnerable to HIV acquisition. In a recent modelling study, the failure to build on existing prevention and treatment coverage gains was found to result in a rebound of the HIV epidemic in the coming years.

1. Introduction

The Southern African HIV Clinicians Society (SAHCS) is a membership organisation of over 3,500 HIV healthcare professionals, including respected figures in the fight against HIV and Tuberculosis (TB) both regionally and internationally. SAHCS was formed in 1998 to promote the highest quality, cost-effective, 'best practice' standard of healthcare for all persons in Southern Africa infected and affected by HIV. For two decades the organisation has assisted in building the capacity of healthcare workers to effectively respond to the epidemic through information dissemination, education and continuing professional development programmes.

As the leading organisation of its kind in the Southern African region, SAHCS has extensive experience and a substantial track record in the co-ordination and facilitation of HIV management training through a variety of mediums, with the most popular being face-to-face lectures and classroom learning. However, this is limiting in the number of healthcare professionals able to attend, especially in the rural areas of the country.

The purpose of the proposed project was for SAHCS to update and transform traditionally classroom-based HIV training into a blended learning experience that is more easily and widely available, adaptable, manageable, and self-sustaining.

Currently, the private healthcare sector is facing an ever-increasing population of HIV-affected patients. The management of these patients and ensuring that they are given the best possible, evidence-based care to ensure their ongoing health and wellbeing is an acknowledged problem in South Africa. There have been several studies conducted which indicated that private sector doctors have difficulty keeping up with the latest developments in how best to manage HIV and its complications (Connolly et al, 1999; Chabikuli et al 2002; Schneider 2005; Innes 2012), and as a result, patients frequently receive inadequate treatment.

In addition, curriculum integration of HIV and AIDS in higher education should be a strategic priority of the country's health systems, yet little progress has been made in this area (Wood & Pillay, 2016). Most medical schools in South and Southern Africa do not provide comprehensive advanced HIV management information, therefore new doctors as well as more experienced public-sector doctors, struggle to managed advanced, complicated and co-infected disease manifestations.

SAHCS wishes to address this skills gap by creating an innovative programme that can reach private sector doctors across South Africa, as well as public sector doctors across the Southern African region, and give them the tools that they need to manage HIV effectively. This will strengthen the healthcare system and promote a healthier society overall.

Traditionally, the Advanced Clinical HIV Management course was run as a ten-day classroom-based training which was an exceptional learning experience, but one that could only be accessed by a handful of doctors – approx. 20 at a time due to work pressures and cost of travel and accommodation in Johannesburg.

SAHCS's ground-breaking concept was to create an interactive, blended learning experience that could be accessed by a much higher volume of course candidates (approx. 500 to 1000 per year). Blended learning is a student-centred approach that combines classroom teaching, and online and technology-based tools. The University of Pretoria quotes research findings that show "that students who are exposed to a hybrid approach outperform students who work in a completely contact or an online only environment".

Whilst cost savings and flexibility are key drivers for the development of blended learning, and will be of significant benefit, the core benefit is to create a learning programme that is widely accessible, stimulating and promotes student engagement and knowledge retention. SAHCS took the well-established, traditionally taught course, and converted it to a self-paced, blended learning experience, with tailored, synchronous virtual classrooms to provide for elements of necessary interactive learning.

This modernisation of the course will facilitate easier access to clinicians operating in rural areas, where the burden of HIV is often high, the health systems are under-resourced and patient outcomes are poor. SAHCS's mission is to 'promote evidence-based, quality HIV healthcare in Southern Africa'. This will result in doctors that stay well informed in a frequently developing field – resulting in a healthier HIV-affected population.

The curriculum consists of 13 modules, including epidemiology, diagnosis, prevention, therapeutics, reproductive health, paediatrics, other special populations, HIV and organ systems, co-morbidities and aging, tuberculosis, and advanced disease. It is a 20-week course (or less), which includes three virtual classrooms, online content, and different modes of assessment, such as oral and written. Learning will be very practical and focus on real-life examples and case studies and will require students to provide input as they move through the course material.

A list of accredited doctors who have graduated from the course can be provided to managed care organisations (medical aids) to facilitate relationship building between them and upskilled practitioners.

2. The infrastructure
Natalie Martyn, SAHCS Programme Manager, listened to Adrian Ziller, Creative Head of Blue Pencil present fascinating data on 'how people learn' at an e-learning convention on 16th March 2017. Through their mutual belief that people should be able to learn in any way they choose, that supports their goals, fires their passions, and lulls them out of complacency; SAHCS and Blue Pencil entered into a contractual agreement to create the first Online Advanced HIV Management Course. Blue Pencil design and develop end-user training content, digital media content, blended learning facilitation, and augmented reality content. Their team consists of learning experts, graffiti artists, sound engineers, multimedia artists, animators, illustrators, and activators that allow them to create the right experience for any situation.

Cornerstone OnDemand (CSOD) was recommended to SAHCS as the "Rolls Royce" of learner management systems. The product prides itself as a unified, cloud platform that enables blended learning in the digital space, connecting with others and accessing content on any device. Cornerstone Connect fosters real-time team collaboration and supports social learning. Cornerstone Learn is the mobile learning app available to all users that provides tools for being productive from anywhere and allows learners to discover new content, pick up where they left off, and continue working through their transcript wherever they are. With offline playback, doctors can download and enjoy content sans internet connection.

Kalleo TalenTek is the authorised reseller and implementation partner for CSOD within South Africa and Africa overall. SAHCS signed a license agreement with Kalleo in September 2017 that would allow the HIV Management Course to be accessed via one of the global leaders in learning systems.

The authors of the clinical training consisted of experienced, specialist research clinicians who have spent their life's work in the field of HIV medicine. Key opinion leaders who are revered globally for their contributions to the advancement of treatment for HIV-positive people collaborated with SAHCS to produce the most up-to-date, evidence-based learning; using SAHCS and World Health Organization (WHO) best practice guidelines and international data.

Other people involved included the CEO, technical editors, a training coordinator, programme manager and SAHCS staff support systems.

3. Challenges

Having never worked in this space before, no amount of medical degrees, MBAs or PhDs could have prepared the project team for the monster of work that lay ahead. e-Learning experts did attempt to shed some light on the complexities of creating online education; but until it became a lived experience, the true meaning of their words fell short. SAHCS is an NPO, that functions broadly as a secretariat, but with a small staff contingent; therefore, with only a Programme Manager and a Training Coordinator managing the process, the initial timeline of twelve months soon morphed into eighteen. Added to this, the initial self-funded budget of R500,000 SAHCS had allocated to building systems and converting content from PowerPoint slides to interactive Articulate Storyline for Cornerstone, ballooned to a staggering R3,000,000.

The majority of doctors who wrote the content provided their services voluntarily outside of normal working hours. This helped significantly towards stemming the tide of overspend. Further to this, SAHCS has submitted funding proposals to managed care organisations such as Discovery Health and the Government Employee Medical Scheme (GEMS), who have shown a keen interest in contributing towards costs. The fees from the course (R5,500 excl. VAT) will show a return on investment within two years.

All online learning must be accurate, but medical-based learning even more so – within the field of HIV, technology and medicine is continuously changing, and as a leader in HIV training, SAHCS has an obligation to ensure its guidelines and training tools are the most current. To this end, some material that was developed at the beginning of the project (March 2017) had to be rewritten or adapted to current data. This has contributed to the delay of releasing the course to doctors. The commitment to keeping the course cutting edge will be an ever-evolving and dedicated process.

Other challenges included a temporary breakdown in relations with Kalleo. Approximately six months into the relationship, SAHCS felt that the level of service and attention required to assist the organisation in navigating this new landscape, was lacking. A high-level meeting was called with the SAHCS CEO, Kalleo MD, Kalleo Sales Director, SAHCS Programme Manager and Blue Pencil's Technical Head. A list of grievances was tabled and after long discussions, Kalleo promised to fulfil their commitment as a service provider to SAHCS and address all concerns raised. Since then, a dedicated Senior Implementation Consultant from Kalleo has been assigned to the SAHCS project and results have improved dramatically.

With regards to the LMS, SAHCS felt that the system itself was not intuitive, much of the design and layout of the customer login page and other functionalities were hard coded and required either payment of significant sums of money to adjust, or they simply could not be changed meaning that the look and feel did not coincide with what SAHCS needed to maintain brand integrity. Since raising these issues, Cornerstone have made a few concessions and improved on the way the system works. Without a doubt, the biggest stumbling block for the project team at SAHCS has been the limited knowledge of digital learning and LMS applications in general. Promising strides have been made as more training has been given, research has been done, and unwavering support provided from Adrian Ziller and his team at Blue Pencil.

Marketing and branding of the course could have been done sooner and with better consultation. Again, lacking the expertise in-house meant that SAHCS did not know to formulate a professional marketing campaign. A marketing and branding consultant was brought in to assist the project team with a robust plan. Since rolling out the strategies recommended, in 6 short months, the SAHCS Facebook page, Twitter account, LinkedIn and Google+ profiles have more than doubled in followers. This gave the HIV course all the traction it needed and approx. 100 doctors per month have enquired about registering.

On the whole, the organisation has had to learn on the go and whilst this has been stressful at times, the overall result is a more knowledgeable, thicker-skinned group of individuals who have a new-found respect for the world of digital learning.

4. How the initiative was received

User Acceptance Testing (UAT) trials took place to test whether the content was viable and whether the system was user-friendly – the first UAT was done by two doctors on 12th March 2018 and the second on 26th March 2018 by five medical doctors, two SAHCS board members, a Health Economist & Risk Manager from Discovery Health, CEO of Iyeza Health, two staff from Blue Pencil, three staff from Kalleo, and the SAHCS CEO.

The initial UAT was largely unsuccessful due to issues with the LMS. This was presented at the meeting with Kalleo and a new plan was designed for the second UAT. The system performed well during this testing. Doctors made detailed notes about changes to content and suggestions about improving user experience. These changes and suggestions have since been implemented.

Since the launch of the marketing campaign in March 2018, over 600 doctors have enquired about the course. 126 doctors have registered and paid. The first release of modules 1 to 7 took place on Tuesday 31st July 2018. The remaining modules 8 to 13 are undergoing international peer-review by a world-renowned infectious disease specialist and will be released at the end of November 2018.

5. Learning outcomes

Whilst SAHCS have yet to measure the full impact of the course, it is the ultimate objective to create a cadre of well-trained HIV experts improving the overall health system and moving rapidly towards achieving 90-90-90, the ambitious treatment target set by UNAIDS to end the epidemic that states, by the year 2020:

- 90% of all people living with HIV will know their HIV status.
- 90% of all people with diagnosed HIV infection will receive sustained antiretroviral therapy.
- 90% of all people receiving antiretroviral therapy will have viral suppression.

(UNAIDS, 2017)

SAHCS will be building a monitoring and evaluation framework to collect data and produce insights into the efficacy of the programme. Cornerstone OnDemand offers powerful and highly configurable custom reports that will contribute to the M&E initiatives.

"I started treating patients with HIV in 1993. I went into private practice in 1994 and became the only GP in central Durban who was willing to assist HIV positive people. I garnered information from journals, medical updates and conferences and kept up to date. Doing this course has been very informative. All in all, the course has helped me iron out grey areas in my knowledge and understanding of HIV and the immune system. I am pleasantly surprised by the depth of the course and am glad I chose to do it, even though it is challenging on my time with work and family commitments" – Dr Aresh Misra (Course participant – private GP)

6. Plans to further develop the initiative

The launch of this course could not be more perfectly timed – South Africa's Health Minister, Dr Aaron Motsoaledi has recently announced plans to implement a National Health Insurance (NHI) which will result in the reconfiguration of the country's healthcare system. When it comes to HIV, South Africa has the highest burden of disease yet a worryingly low percentage of qualified clinicians who can treat it. HIV is not taught extensively in med school and until now, the onus has fallen largely on the public sector to tackle the epidemic. With the NHI rolling out, doctors in the private sector will see massively increased numbers of patients who are HIV-positive and will be required by the National Department of Health and medical aids to manage the disease effectively. Online, and own time access to a 20-week training course that is fully accredited will fast track this process significantly. The continued development of up-to-date content for doctors will remain a priority throughout the lifetime of this course.

SAHCS has launched with a very viable product but over time will replicate the project across different sectors and include emerging technologies such as augmented reality, infographics, support tools, just-enough-just-in time learning, podcasts, animation, and video; in order to stay relevant in a rapidly changing market.

The potential to scale is evident in the initial responses to the advertising of the doctor's course – since the organisation does not exclusively cater to doctors; nurses and other healthcare workers have been begging for a similar course that addresses their needs. Nurses sit at the coalface of the epidemic and are the first point of contact for most HIV-positive people at primary healthcare facilities across the country. Plans are also afoot to de-schedule ARVs so that pharmacists can dispense and prescribe these medicines without the patient needing to see a doctor first. This will require a full-scale, nationwide training initiative that can only be achieved through easier access to education.

According to the Health Professions Council of South Africa, more than 37,300 doctors are registered in the country and almost 12,300 of them are qualified as specialists. There are 287,079 male and female nurses (South African Nursing Council (SANC), 2017), and 14,932 pharmacists. SAHCS's plan is to adapt the Advanced HIV Management course so that this untapped resource of nurses, clinical associates, pharmacists and other healthcare workers can be reached, and given access to the same high-quality training that will support their roles and ensure the proper treatment and continuum of care is delivered to people living with HIV.

"Knowledge is an essential component of the armaments needed to fight HIV. This course will provide you with that essential weapon" – Dr Moeketsi Mathe (Board member, SAHCS and course participant)

7. The future of healthcare is digital
On Friday 1st June 2018, 200 people sat inside the conference halls of the Interest Workshop in Rwanda, at a debate where Prof Francois Venter argued that technology interventions will not end the HIV epidemic in Africa.

Except that it might help.

The digital health market is set to exceed USD 379 billion by 2024 (IDDNA, 2017) - the number of smartphone users in South Africa is expected to reach over 25 million by 2022 (Statista, 2018). With a population of 56 million, that is more than half the country's citizens walking around with a tiny computer in their back pocket. Rising cost cutting pressures in the healthcare industry generates a requirement for providers to seek mobile health technologies for health monitoring thereby, saving large amounts of healthcare costs.

If SAHCS, a leading HIV-training organisation in Southern Africa, does not get onboard with this approaching wave of tech, doctors and healthcare providers will seek the consumption of knowledge elsewhere, as it becomes more readily and widely available. In this industry, SAHCS holds the competitive advantage – it would be short-sighted, and dangerous to the relevance of the organisation not to embrace the advances in e-Learning and to become experts not only in science & medicine, but in the way that knowledge is delivered. Technology itself will not end the HIV epidemic in Africa, but in order for our world-class, globally

Natalie Martyn

recognised clinical training to reach the country's under-resourced and poorly trained healthcare professionals; technology can be a powerful tool and is needed now more than ever.

References

Chabikuli, et al. Quality and equity of private sector care for sexually transmitted diseases in South Africa. Health Policy Plan. 2002 Dec;17 Suppl:40-6.

Connolly, et al. Inadequate Treatment for Sexually Transmitted Diseases in the South African Private Health Sector. Int J STD AIDS. 1999 May;10(5):324-7.

Schneider, H. Sexually transmitted infections – factors associated with quality of care amongst private general practitioners. S Afr Med J. 2005 Oct;95(10):782-5.

Innes, C. A novel HIV treatment model using private practitioners in South Africa. Sex Transm Infect. 2012 Mar; 88(2): 136–140.

IDDNA. (2017, October 07). Digital Health - The Future of Healthcare | EIS Investment. Retrieved from IDDNA Switzerland: https://idna.works/blog/corporate/digital-health-future-healthcare

South African Nursing Council (SANC). (2017, December 31). South African Nursing Council. Retrieved from Annual Statistics: http://www.sanc.co.za/stats_an.htm

Statista. (2018). Number of smartphone users in South Africa from 2014 to 2022 (in millions). Retrieved from The Statistics Portal: https://www.statista.com/statistics/488376/forecast-of-smartphone-users-in-south-africa/

UNAIDS. (2017, January 01). 90–90–90 - An ambitious treatment target to help end the AIDS epidemic. Retrieved from UNAIDS: http://www.unaids.org/en/resources/documents/2017/90-90-90

Wood, L., & Pillay, M. (2016). A review of HIV and AIDS curricular respones in the higher education sector: Where are we now and what next? South African Journal of Higher Education, 126-143.

Author Biography

Natalie Martyn studied Health Sciences at the Australian College of Natural Medicine in 2002 and in 2017, completed a Management Advancement Programme with the Wits Business School in South Africa. Natalie has been working at the Southern African HIV Clinicians Society for 12 years. As a Programme Manager her role is to oversee grant-funded projects and implement strategies to improve profitability for the organisation, which is currently moving from a completely donor-funded business model, to a social enterprise structure.

www.ingramcontent.com/pod-product-compliance
Lightning Source LLC
Chambersburg PA
CBHW072244270326
41930CB00010B/2262